PARADISE

Seems So Far

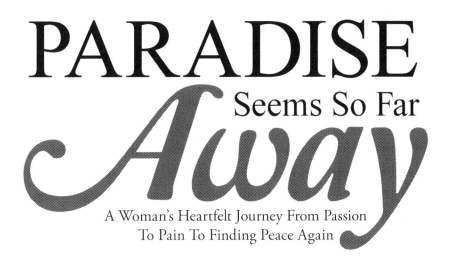

A Woman's Heartfelt Journey From Passion
To Pain To Finding Peace Again

ASHLYN LARK

WESTBOW
PRESS®
A DIVISION OF THOMAS NELSON
& ZONDERVAN

Cover Art by Daria Doyle Renaissance Gallery
www.dariadoyle.com

Scripture taken from the Holy Bible, NEW INTERNATIONAL VERSION®. Copyright © 1973, 1978, 1984 by Biblica, Inc. All rights reserved worldwide. Used by permission. NEW INTERNATIONAL VERSION® and NIV® are registered trademarks of Biblica, Inc. Use of either trademark for the offering of goods or services requires the prior written consent of Biblica US, Inc.

WestBow Press books may be ordered through booksellers or by contacting:

WestBow Press
A Division of Thomas Nelson & Zondervan
1663 Liberty Drive
Bloomington, IN 47403
www.westbowpress.com
1 (866) 928-1240

ISBN: 978-1-5127-0461-7 (sc)
ISBN: 978-1-5127-0462-4 (hc)
ISBN: 978-1-5127-0460-0 (e)

Library of Congress Control Number: 2015913604

Print information available on the last page.

WestBow Press rev. date: 7/20/2016

DEDICATION

This book is dedicated to my first-born child,
my beautiful daughter, Celia,
who was a victim of childhood hardships,
but is now a survivor who,
by the grace and strength of our Lord and Savior
Jesus Christ, has grown into a lovely woman.

PARADISE
Song by:
Ashlyn Lark

Paradise, it seems so far away
Paradise, a thousand years is as a day
Well I know that you are there, my precious little one
Shining bright in the light of the sun

Paradise, where flowers never die
I know it's paradise, but I still wonder why
Why did you go so soon?
Why aren't you here with me?
How I wish my heart could hear
I wish my eyes could see
You in paradise, but it seems so far away
Paradise, I'll be with you in paradise someday

I will run to you
I will never let you go
And as I hold you close to me
Then I will know, yes, then I will know

Paradise, where streets are paved with gold
Paradise, where we will never grow old

CONTENTS

FOREWORD

By Rosemary Barnes

In a time when there is so much pain and woundedness in our culture, Ashlyn Lark, in her book, *Paradise Seems So Far Away*, has presented her life story with creativity and a perspective that points to the only answer, a loving God. Into a description of her circumstances, she weaves her own poetry and songs that express so well her heart's journey. I feel that other women who are experiencing difficult situations in their own lives, will be encouraged by Ashlyn's honest words, her creativity, but most especially her presentation of her loving Father, Who promises to "never leave you or forsake you…" (Hebrews 13:5) and Who "… is our refuge and strength, a very present help in times of trouble." (Psalm 46:1). What could be more uplifting and comforting to know that our God is in control of our lives, even in the darkest times!

Author and Speaker Rosemary Barnes

PROLOGUE

Fire to My Soul

There are not many people who bring fire to your soul by just their words or presence. The Holy Scriptures, my loving husband Paul, and my best friend Amy are of the few that have that effect on me. While collaborating with Amy on this project, she said, "You know, this book is not for you, it's a sequence of events in your life that have been brought together to be used by God to minister to many different people." These words of truth lit a flame inside of me and brought to light many revelations. It is my prayer that through my trials, triumphs, and lessons you will be enlightened and encouraged, ultimately giving you a lasting faith in God's love and power. I believe God can sustain you through life's turbulence and heal your deepest hurts.

From the depths of my soul as a poet and songwriter, writing this book was more difficult than I had ever imagined. As I gathered all of the poetry I had written over the years and relived my daughter's life, death, and funeral, my heart ached even more for her. I also felt great compassion for the many women who can truly identify with my pain. For many years, it has been my heart's desire to share my story and testimony of faith, healing, and restoration. Finally, in God's perfect timing, He has given me the strength to complete it. It is my hopeful prayer that no matter what you have experienced in your life, you will trust that God is always there to hold you in His arms, provide for all your needs and carry you through the storms. He did this for me and, as I give Him all the glory, I am eternally grateful.

All poetry and songs were written by Ashlyn Lark, copyright 2012

CHAPTER 1

Destined to Meet

Looks Can Be Deceiving; Things Are Not Always What They Appear To Be.

But each one is tempted when, by his own evil
desires, he is dragged away and enticed.
—James 1:14

They say when autumn leaves fall from the trees you should be ready to embrace the season's changes. I always believed this cliché. Even in my childhood, significant changes seemed to blow into my life at that time of year. Sometimes, those changes were cool and refreshing, like a dip in the ocean on a hot summer day. Sometimes they were as beautiful as a flower blossoming with the fragrance of spring. Other times the changes were harsh and cold like a furious winter storm. I have always been a sensitive soul, anticipating the next season and longing for the beauty that it could bring.

In this particular time of my life, spring had sprung, with its fresh air and flowers blooming everywhere. I was a young, naive bride in my early twenties, and I had married my best friend. On the outside, we appeared to be a happy, vivacious couple. However, on the inside, I was restless and still searching for something more, especially because the chemistry between us was somehow missing.

We worked together at an exclusive health spa where we proudly displayed the image of Barbie and Ken. I was an aerobics teacher, and Don was a personal trainer and weight-room manager. He was an outstanding athlete, and when he wasn't participating in some kind of sport, he was watching one on TV. Even though I knew of his passion for athletics before I married him, I was disheartened from his lack of interest and passion for me as his wife. But I must admit that much of the time, I was selfishly focused on *my* needs being met rather than what I could give to the marriage relationship.

Our friendship was strong, but my longing for romance and my disappointment in our love life only intensified with time. I opened my heart by communicating my needs and desires to him, especially my yearning to hear words of affirmation. This was my love language, and he just wasn't speaking it. He told me that he didn't need to compliment me, because other people did. Since most of Don's time and energy went into sports, he had little left for our marriage. I could have walked in front of the television in a skimpy nightgown, and I'm sure he would've asked me to move out of the way. He wouldn't want to miss his sports entertainment! Because he was so consumed, I filled my spare time with creative activities like decorating our home and art projects. But loneliness and disappointing thoughts about what a marriage was supposed to be still permeated my heart.

At times, it seemed like we were living two separate lives. My attempts to bring us closer were only bandages on an already broken marriage. I flirted with the idea that surely there must be someone out there who would be captivated by me. I was a damsel in distress; only in this fairy tale, I was trapped in a tower surrounded by playoff games and sports highlights!

After three years of feeling emotionally abandoned, bored, and resentful, I finally threw in the proverbial towel. My love tank was empty. Divorce seemed to be the only way out and was a common solution to marital dissatisfaction. The grass did look greener on the other side, and I wanted to run through it barefoot, wild, and free! However, there can be danger and deception in exploring new territories when your heart is left carelessly unguarded. Nothing could have prepared me for the extreme peaks and valleys I was about to endure in the next season of my life.

One beautiful summer morning, everything began to change. Now in my mid-twenties, I continued to work as an aerobics instructor while pursuing a professional modeling career. I did not consider myself anywhere near the top of the ladder in the modeling arena; my résumé was only slightly impressive. My work included seven TV commercials, an ad for suntan lotion, and print work for various brochures, catalogs, and advertising. These were my only claim to fame, but I enjoyed the excitement and the glamorous milieu. At that time, I was also a singer and songwriter and had performed in various bands. Music was my passion, but not my profession.

On that particular morning, I was caught in traffic on my way to a very important casting call. When I arrived at the hotel, I realized I was late for my appointment, which totally stressed me out. As I quickly ran across the street, an extremely attractive older man caught my eye. He was sharply dressed and carrying what appeared to be a black briefcase. We stared at each other intently; I was mesmerized. This initial attraction was definitely the lust of the eyes and of the flesh!

Thank goodness, I had the chance to pull myself together in the elevator on my way up to the suite where the casting was being held. When I entered the room, I was a little flustered but felt confident wearing my favorite teal outfit. I sat down and waited with the other models until it was my turn to show the clients my portfolio. What I didn't know was that they already had selected me for this job along with a European male model named Andre. The clients had carefully matched our headshots together from more than one hundred composites for a brochure promoting a new resort on a Caribbean island.

During my interview, there was an expression of disappointment on their faces. I had cut several inches off my long, blonde hair and because I was late, the model they had chosen to work with me had already left. They wanted to see us together in person. The clients informed me that if they decided they still wanted to use me, my agency would be in touch. As my heart sank, I said thank-you, grabbed my portfolio, and left. At that point, I wished I had left my hair the way it was in most of my photos.

The next day, I received a phone call from my agent. To my surprise, they still wanted me for this job despite the issues. I was thrilled! I couldn't believe it. I would spend one week shooting a brochure on an exotic island. They told me that the first three days I would be alone with my "model husband." The last four days, we would be shooting with other models who would be flying in. They gave me details about what to pack for my wardrobe and told me there would be a makeup artist and hairstylist on the set. This was a great gig!

My agent later informed me that I was booked for another shoot on the same day that I would be flying out. It would be tight, but it was hard to refuse a job for a major jean company that involved two hunky bodybuilders. The first booking was scheduled for the morning, so I would have to leave immediately afterward to catch my flight. I had a lot to do in preparation for the trip. Most importantly, I needed to go by my agency to pick up Andre's composite, the model that would be acting as my future husband. I couldn't wait to see what he looked like.

On the day of our departure, he would be waiting for me at the airport at a specific time with our airplane tickets. The only way we would be able to find each other would be by our photo composites. I was very curious and excited to meet my pretend husband. I wondered if our encounter would be one of serendipity. Don's face began to completely fade from my memory.

The night preceding the trip, I had a hard time falling asleep. I had picked up Andre's composite. To say he was strikingly gorgeous in his photos was an understatement. I wanted to impress him and look my very best. It wasn't unusual for the artist in me to be awakened late at night, so I got out of bed and used my anxious energy to design something new to wear on the flight with Andre.

When I was a little girl, my mother taught me how to sew. As a young adult, I attempted getting a degree in fashion design, but headed for the door when one of the classes required a mathematical mind. For an extremely right-brained person, the challenge was unthinkable, but creativity came naturally to me.

I ended up sewing all night, and into the wee hours of the morning, confident my new outfit was a success. With only a few hours of sleep, I headed off to my first shoot of the day. I was late again after getting lost, but the photographer was kind and patient. This was before cell phones! The shoot was a blast, and the photographer got the look he wanted for the ad. Then I was on my way (on time!) to the airport to meet my Andre.

Upon arrival, suitcase in one hand and the photo in the other, I began to search for this man. It didn't take long to spot him—he looked like he belonged on the cover of a *GQ* magazine. After introducing ourselves, we couldn't help but feel a bit awkward in this unusual rendezvous. I felt like I was in a movie with James Bond; he was tall, distinguished looking, confident, and well mannered. His appearance was a stark contrast to my free-spirited, artsy look, which was apparent in my newly made outfit. I felt a little anxious due to my lack of worldly experience and the fact that I had never met this man before!

His demeanor was very suave. He was eloquent in his speech and had a very sexy accent. He treated me like a lady by opening doors for me, and he acted as if we were already a couple. I felt flattered by his unwavering attention.

As we were boarding the plane, we both realized this was not our first encounter. He was the man who had caught my eye and exchanged that intriguing glance. It hadn't been a briefcase in his hand—it was his modeling portfolio. We had crossed each other's path outside the hotel where the casting was being held without knowing we had already been matched together. Now, though we were complete strangers, we were traveling together as a couple. We had been chosen for each other as if in an arranged marriage.

During the flight, our conversation was so engaging that I soon became mesmerized by his demure manner. I was finding myself more and more captivated by his presence. When we arrived on the island, it seemed like a whole different world to us. The airport was chaotic. It was filled with crazy, loud passengers trying to communicate, jockeying for position at the crowded luggage carrousels. We couldn't wait to get to the hotel. We took a taxi to the property, winding through the busy city, and out to the lush, open fields, marveling at the beauty of the landscape. We could see the resort in the distance. It was magnificent. The tropical plants and exotic flowers that surrounded the property were breathtaking.

The inside of the hotel was even more impressive with its inviting island décor. As the ocean breeze swept through the open archways of the lobby, the sun welcomed us with its tangible warmth. My room was charming with a bamboo canopy bed and an enchanting view of the ocean. The tranquil sound of the waves was soothing to the soul.

After settling into our rooms, we met with the clients in the lobby. They discussed the schedule and locations for the photo shoot for the week. They also told us we would be on our own for meals until the other models arrived a few days later. After that meeting, we went exploring the hotel in search of a restaurant where we would have dinner that evening. We found the perfect spot; it was a secluded outdoor setting among the tropics. The restaurant was amazing, with incredible, enormous terracotta pots filled with exotic red anthuriums and blooming birds of paradise. I had never seen anything like it before.

After watching a picturesque sunset, the full moon illuminated the restaurant, adding to its unique ambiance. It was enchanting to say the least. As we were dancing to some familiar tunes played by a calypso band, he briefly left me on the dance floor. I was awestruck when he returned with an exotic flower and placed it in my hair. Andre put me on a pedestal and made me feel like a goddess. The admiration and attention he gave me was a complete contrast to the way I was treated by Don. The chemistry between us was amazingly intense as we flirted playfully for the rest of the evening. Despite the innate attraction between us, he remained a gentleman. Andre walked me back to my room and gave me a kiss good night on the cheek. As I tried to go to sleep, thoughts of this romantic evening filled my senses and captured my entire being. I wondered if it was love or lust? All I knew was that I couldn't wait to see him again.

In the morning, the first photo shoot was taken at the beach. We walked along the shore in our swimsuits holding hands. Then they shot us playing tennis and golf. During the shoot on the golf course, we were caught in a sudden downpour of rain. We ran as fast as we could to our golf cart and then almost crashed going down a hill as we rushed back toward the hotel. Completely drenched, we laughed hysterically as this adventure added to the excitement of our day. We shared an ongoing quest for more than just an imitation of a magical romance. The mystique of our passionate indulgence was almost taboo.

The final shot was taken at sunset. As we gazed into each other's eyes, we seductively held a glass of wine with our right arms entangled as one. We made a toast for the photographer and to our own decadence. We were at the most elegant, romantic restaurant in the resort, sitting on the terrace of a chateau overlooking the ocean. It was like a day in Utopia. I felt as if

I had been swept away by the man of my dreams. Andre was winning me over with his looks, charm and constant flattery. He knew the game of pursuit and strategically played it well!

That night Andre and I had dinner at a very intimate upscale restaurant. Still entranced by the dynamic chemistry between us, our conversation became more engaging. As love songs whispered seductive melodies from a grand piano, our appetite for each other subconsciously increased. That evening, the boundaries of our flesh were weakened. He won me over and captured more than just my heart.

The rest of the week went by quickly, especially after the other models arrived. The women were very attractive and even though I had been chosen as the main model for the ad, I was still intimidated by them. One model kept flirting with Andre and enticing the other male models. She was invading what was becoming my territory. In spite of this, the crew had fun together and shared some lasting memories. Every time I hear the song "Yellow Bird up High in Banana Tree," it reminds me of our last evening on the island. We stayed up very late celebrating and singing the night away.

Another memory I have of this trip was of spiritual significance. One of the models had his wife flown in to celebrate their ten-year anniversary. One evening at dinner she shared her testimony. She explained how she had suffered with severe depression in the past and how Jesus healed her and set her free. She was a "born-again Christian," and her favorite symbol was the butterfly, signifying the metamorphosis of one's new life in Christ. She was even wearing a shirt with butterflies on it. As she "preached" to us about reading the Bible, she told us we needed to ask Jesus into our hearts. As she spoke, her husband became increasingly embarrassed, cutting her off and trying to change the subject. I personally didn't understand where she was coming from, but I was curious about the joy she illuminated and the peace she had found. I now understand that there is an evident transformation when you become a new creature in Christ. There is a supernatural birth of the spirit and a hunger for the things of God.

At this time of my life, I was spiritually lost. I explored different avenues of new age philosophies, but they all seemed to be deceiving. None of them satisfied my longing for a supernatural experience of fulfillment. I was living for my own desires, seeking pleasure in the things of this world.

I had little interest in the things of God. My divorce from Don was not yet finalized and I was getting passionately involved with a man I barely knew. Andre had already told me he loved me and we both entertained the thought that it was our destiny to be together forever. After only one week of knowing each other, that was a very dangerous and foolish assumption! Andre persuaded me to speed up the divorce process and finalize it as quickly as possible. He had been married before and assured me that even though divorce was painful, the quicker it was finalized the better. I was waiting for the final court date to be done with it.

On our flight back, we reminisced of the surreal experience that held our hearts captive. At the end of our conversation, he proudly placed a love letter in my hand. One he had secretly written to me before our connecting flight. These were his words:

October 7, 1986 5:45

My Dearest and Beautiful Love Ashlyn,

I love you so much. My love is so intense that sometimes, just looking in your eyes can make me cry. I feel that your love is so precious, so sensitive, and so pure it could make me melt. I am so proud of our love. I want us to love each other more and more everyday of our lives until the day we die with that same pure intensity. I am going to marry you, have children with you and be with you forever!

Andre

My heart was flaming with desire, while my mind was lost in the land of infatuation. Beware … love too fast or too soon can be deceiving. Do not give your heart away so easily.

CHAPTER 2

Trying to Fill the Emptiness

Stop Stuffing the World into the God-Shaped Hole in Your Heart.

Jesus answered, "I am the Way, and the Truth, and the
Life. No one comes to The Father except through Me."
John 14:6

After returning home, our love affair became such an obsession that it seemed like an eternity whenever we were apart. We decided the torture of not being together was too much. The desires of our flesh were so compelling that we couldn't live apart any longer. Andre lived in a condominium on the beach with a lovely view of the ocean. I willingly moved in. We celebrated this union with discussions of a future marriage, with two or three children, spending the rest our lives together in total bliss.

During the first week of living with Andre, he told me that if he ever had a daughter he wanted to name her Celia. His passion about this name came from one of his favorite songs. As he sang it for me, I was touched by its soothing tone. Its melody was captivating and the lyrics moved me to tears. The song told the story of a young woman named Celia who had beautiful blue eyes but they were often saddened with tears. When her parents passed away, she made many sacrifices and ultimately gave up her life to raise her younger siblings. Although she was engaged to a wonderful man, Celia chose to put the needs of her precious family first. We both agreed that if we ever had a daughter we would definitely give her this name, which means heavenly.

As we settled into living together, it was difficult adjusting to all of the changes. I missed the home Don and I had bought together. I decorated it with my own personal touch, so when I left, it felt like I was leaving a piece of myself behind. What bothered me the most was my conscience, struggling with guilt for breaking Don's heart. He was crushed when I left him, but never tried to save the marriage or keep it alive when I told him I wanted out. He just let me go without a fight. We both lacked commitment and the desire to make it work.

My family adored Don's gentle personality, so they thought I had totally lost my mind for ending the marriage and moving in with Andre not long after. They still loved me unconditionally, but found it difficult understanding my irrational behavior. What made it even more upsetting was that my father was very ill. He was suffering with a cancerous brain tumor that was inoperable. My family was consumed and devastated by his condition. Their main focus and energy was directed toward my father who was approaching the end of his life.

Before his cancer diagnosis, my parents had just purchased a new home. Prior to that, they lived in the same house for thirty years. This was the house I grew up in. I was the seventh of eight children. There were two boys and six girls. Most of my childhood memories were made in that house on West 63rd Street. I can remember my mother saying, "If these walls could talk, what stories they would tell!" These memories inspired me to write the following poem.

The House on 63rd Street

So vivid I see the memories,
Still taunting me in my sleep,
Of childhood days and feelings that remain,
Of growing up on 63rd Street.
A family of ten members,
All gathered together as one,
Enduring much love and pain,
With six daughters and two older sons.
I recall my mother's stern voice,
She struggled with crippled hands and feet,
Often calling upon the Lord for strength,
In the house on 63rd Street.

My father worked so hard to provide for a home,
Which wasn't always a haven,
With eight kids to clothe and feed,
There wasn't much money left for savin'.
He was gentle and full of mercy,
But stress had taken its toll,
I recall him crying out in his anguish,
Lord God have mercy on my soul.
Many babies' first steps were taken,
In that house on 63rd Street,
Many tender hearts were bruised,
Sung to and rocked to sleep.

The sharing of joys and laughter,
Were almost outnumbered by tears,
There were many trials and hardships,
Through the seasons of the years.
So many secrets and sorrows,
In that house where I would dwell,
And if the walls could talk,
They wouldn't just whisper, they would yell!

11

From tricycles to bicycles,
To motorcycles and cars,
Time flew us through the years,
Leaving many memories and scars.

For every place where your heart dwells,
Every person that shares your path,
Captures a part of your soul,
As the wind blows away the chaff.

My father received his pilot's license in the Air Force during World War II. Thankfully he never had to go into combat. After the war, he worked as a co-pilot for a commercial airline and then took a position as an air traffic controller, which he ended up doing for the next twenty-seven years. It was a very stressful job, with constant schedule changes wreaking havoc on his emotional and physical health. All of this stress, coupled with coming home to a house full of eight children, was overwhelming! My mom tried to keep the law and order as my dad was completely burnt out. He was an intelligent man and worked hard to provide for his family.

One of my fondest memories of my dad was when I was very young. He used to pretend he was landing an airplane on a runway as he drove the family station wagon down the block toward our house. My sisters and I thought it was really cool and a lot of fun to imagine. I was always proud of the fact that he could pilot a plane. But those days were long gone, taken away by the mystery of time and the affliction of his disease.

He was extremely frail in the last weeks of his life. I hated seeing him suffer from the treatments of chemotherapy and radiation. These methods only made him worse and caused him to deteriorate more rapidly. I knew our time together was fleeting, so each visit was precious to me. Because we had such a large family, I was rarely alone with him. During his last days in the hospital, God provided me that opportunity. As I sat beside him, I witnessed something I will never forget. My dad looked up at the ceiling and stared intensely. It was as if someone was speaking to him. A peace came over him; I could see it in his eyes. He appeared to be having some sort of vision. As I leaned toward him he whispered softly, "Ashlyn, do you see them?" I replied, "No Daddy, I don't. What is it that you see?"

Before he had the chance to answer, a nurse entered the room interrupting the moment to check his vital signs. I couldn't help but wonder if he had a spiritual encounter with angels or if he was hallucinating from the pain medicine. He had such peace; I wondered if God allowed him to have a glimpse of Heaven.

On my next visit to see him, it was heart wrenching to see how he had deteriorated so quickly. He cried and begged me to take him home to die. My mother was on her way to the hospital; when she arrived I pleaded with her privately to respect my father's request. I knew it would be hard for her to take care of him because of her life-long crippling arthritis. My dad always helped take care of her, doing some of the tasks that she was physically incapable of doing. My older siblings also helped with daily chores and taking care of the younger children. My father even called us the big ones and the little ones.

Soon after telling my mother how he expressed to me his wishes to die at home, she did honor his request and agreed to sign the papers for him to be released that day. With the help of hospice and family members, we took care of him at home for the remainder of his life.

Not long after his return home, our family gathered around my father's bed as he took his last breath. My mother spoke through her tears, saying to my father, "I love you, darling." I never once heard my mother call him by his first name. She always used sweet words of endearment like "dear," "honey" and "darling." She was devastated from the loss of her companion of nearly fifty years. He was the love of her life. After seeing him suffer so severely, I was convinced that dying from cancer was one of the worst ways to go.

Adding to my mother's grief was the worry that her daughter was living with a man she hardly knew. I was so blinded and mesmerized by Andre that nothing else seemed to matter. After my father's death, I clung to Andre even more. My emotions led me to believe that he would fulfill everything that was missing in my life. He was all I had ever dreamed of and all that I would ever need. After all, we were madly in love and this was our destiny!

Losing my father was an insufferable process, yet I found solace and comfort in being with an older man because he gave me a sense of strength and security. At times he seemed overly possessive, but I blindly ignored it. Other times he was a soft place to fall. I was longing to fill the emptiness that was aching deep inside of me. I didn't realize that my soul was really crying out for more than what this man could ever give me - a supernatural encounter with the lover of my soul, Jesus.

As our relationship progressed, our obsession for each other intensified. We became insanely jealous. He was flirtatious with other women, even in front of me. Because of the nature of our careers, we feared that someone or something would come between us. While the modeling jobs I was getting were non-threatening, Andre was getting a lot of jobs that left me feeling insecure. I was fearful of losing our magical bond of love. I wanted to trust him but he seemed to be enjoying himself far too much. It made me wonder if he would be tempted by all the attention he was getting from the other models. After all, that's how we met and fell in love.

One of the bookings he had was for a perfume company. It was a seductive TV commercial filmed in a bedroom setting with Miss Venezuela. Another was a photo shoot for a major cruise line where he took off for three days with a model named Monica. I had seen her before at castings; she was drop-dead gorgeous. His flirtatious personality was alarming even when he wasn't working. I tried to keep my thoughts to myself, but I couldn't bear the thought of losing him. These jobs were causing a destructive path of conflict. We finally realized that if we were going to survive as a couple, our modeling careers had to come to an end.

Before I worked as a model or in a health spa, I had worked part-time as a floral designer. I always loved the arts and enjoyed many forms of creative expression. I decided to search for a full-time position at a flower shop. I ended up working at a large shop not too far from where I lived. I eventually became a manager for the design room and helped with the window displays. I enjoyed expressing my artistic gifts in this type of work. Most of the designers were nice to me, but nothing is ever perfect. The majority of employees at this large shop did not speak English very well. After losing my father, and feeling isolated from my family, this environment only added to my grief and frustration. Even though there was a language barrier, I hung in there because we needed the income. After Andre quit modeling, he ambitiously started a male modeling agency. Without a paycheck from this new business, I began to resent being the sole provider while he poured himself into his new venture.

As time passed, our minds were awakened to many truths. The rose colored glasses we once wore had turned into dark shades of gray. We were both disappointed in each other. The expectations we had envisioned for our relationship were not being met. Our perfect love affair in reality was just an illusion. We still cared deeply for one another, but time was revealing the deception of instant love. The honeymoon stage of our relationship was beginning to wear off.

They say opposites attract but we started to realize how extremely different our personalities were. Andre was very eccentric, intense and high-strung, while I was more mellow, introverted and easygoing. In the beginning of our relationship, he was attracted to the idea that I was more like him - confident, determined and driven. He knew I had high ambitions of becoming a recording artist. He was impressed with me and proud of my talents. Prior to meeting Andre, I had the opportunity to go to Los Angeles and New York with my music producer to pitch two of my original songs. At that time of my life, I wrote the following song about making it in the music business, which was my greatest hope.

I'm Gonna' Fly

(Verse One)
I'm a waitin' for that lucky break,
Sitting on the edge of my seat,
I'm a prayin' that I've got what it takes,
For someone to discover me.
I've been runnin' 'round this crazy wheel,
Like a hamster in a cage,
Same 'ol story the same 'ol lines,
I'm ready to turn the page.

(Chorus)
I'm gonna' climb to the mountain top,
I'm gonna' give it everything I've got,
I'm gonna' fly where the eagles soar,
There's nothing that I want more.

(Verse Two)
I don't want to keep my feet on the ground,
I'll be dancin' in the clouds,
You might even get my autograph,
If you can make it through the crowds.
A fancy wardrobe beyond my dreams,
My name will be up in lights,
A limo waitin' behind the scenes,
I'll shine like a star in the night.

After all the rejection from record companies, I lost my passion for pursuing this seemingly far-fetched dream. But to Andre I had become a quitter. He acted very disappointed in me giving up on my aspirations. Many other things did not meet his expectations, which left me feeling like a failure and very inadequate. I wondered if I could ever be good enough for him. He started picking on the little things I did, accusing me of not listening to him. He even became verbally abusive, telling me I was stupid and couldn't do anything right. He started to show patterns of anger and withdrawal, not speaking to me for days. He wanted to control every part of my life and isolate me from my family and friends. He had become very possessive of me. I had low self-esteem and was more of an introvert, which made me an easy target for his abuse. I wanted to fit into the mold he had made for me but I knew deep inside God had designed me in a different way. At times, he had a tender heart and I believed he still loved me. I was afraid of losing even a fraction of that love. After all, we had already gone this far into the relationship and our soul tie was much too strong to sever.

It was extremely difficult for me to deal with his perfectionism and meticulous ways as well as his tendency to be a control freak. Sometimes he was very arrogant and prideful. When we had a disagreement, he would often lose his temper and curse at me. His thoughtless words crushed my spirit and made me feel worthless. These outbursts of anger were usually followed by days of withdrawal. When the storms blew over, we seemed to patch things up but I was left wounded by the debris. I still loved him and wanted to make it work. Furthermore, I loved the fact that he absolutely had no interest in football. He did like tennis, so we played occasionally and took long walks on the beach to stay in shape. He was a trained chef and used his culinary skills to delight me with many delicious meals and desserts. I didn't like to cook, so I was grateful for that.

After being together for almost a year, my mother kept insisting we set a wedding date. With her persuasion and our commitment to each other, we decided to move forward in the relationship. I began searching everywhere in countless malls and boutiques to find the perfect wedding dress to fit my bohemian style. When I married Don, I had designed and fashioned my own wedding gown. This time I didn't want to take on such a tedious task. After a mad search and much disappointment in not finding the right one, I ended up settling on something that Andre had selected for me. It was a lacey skirt and blouse outfit. Even though it wasn't typically me, it was still lovely. It was made with an ivory-colored silk fabric overlaid with various patterns of lace. The flowers, on the other hand, were designed to my perfection. I wore a halo of white roses with baby's breath, which encircled my wavy blond sun-streaked hair. My bridal bouquet matched my headpiece but had an added touch of larkspur.

We had a simple ceremony that was performed by a female Justice of the Peace. Our only guests were my mother, one of Andre's sisters, and a dear friend and her husband. My friend was working toward becoming a professional photographer. She generously offered to take our pictures at no charge as a wedding gift to us. She captured many amazing moments as we walked down to the beach barefoot to exchange our wedding vows. It was beautiful. We did end up celebrating with my family at a later date.

The passion we felt for each other was so intense, it became the glue that held us together through the storms of our relationship. Andre's passion revealed itself in many forms. He had little tolerance for anyone who did not share his opinions or idiosyncrasies, especially me. He definitely showed signs of narcissism. He was extremely annoyed by our differences and at times made that very clear to me. The other side to his passion was eccentric and very ugly. After we were married, his attacks were not only verbal and emotional but he also started becoming physically abusive. In the heat of one argument, he even pushed me against the wall. Another time, he physically forced me out the door of our apartment. I couldn't believe he would treat me like this, and I started to become afraid of him. As terrible as these episodes were, I believed that he would change and be overpowered by my love. As terrified as I was, I ignored these warning signs that his temper could escalate and get much worse. I tried to focus on the good in our marriage, and stay committed even though I knew this was an unhealthy relationship.

I had compassion for him because of the difficult times he experienced in his childhood. His father was a strict disciplinarian who believed in severe methods of punishment. After one episode of disobedience, his father sent him away to live at a monastery when he was a young child. Feeling alone and rejected, he cried himself to sleep at night. He seldom had any visitors and when he finally returned back home, he harbored deep feelings of resentment for being sent away.

Before this traumatic experience, his newborn baby sister whom he loved dearly had become very ill. His mother was getting into the car with the baby, to rush her to the hospital when Andre frantically ran towards them, desperately wanting to hug his baby sister goodbye. In the confusion of the moment, his grandfather abruptly pushed him away, not allowing him even a final glimpse of her little face. She never returned back home. This loss created a deep scar of emptiness that he carried into his adult life. The trials he suffered caused him to harbor a spirit of rejection and a fear of abandonment. Even though there was no excuse for his volatile behavior toward me, I tried to understand where these cycles were coming from. I knew how much this man was affected by these deep wounds from his childhood.

When conflicts occurred, I wanted to resolve them immediately but this only angered him more. I ended up feeling isolated waiting for the storm to pass. I walked on eggshells hoping I didn't do something to provoke him further. They say the apple doesn't fall far from the tree and this was a classic example. Andre was repeating the abusive behavior he experienced from his father. Similarly, I was just like his mother - trapped. How I longed to find peace.

> *We all chase after the wind. It is part of our human frailty. Yet when we chase after God, we find serenity. No one and nothing on this earth can satisfy that longing. Only God can.*

CHAPTER 3

A Pink Surprise

Children Are a Blessing.

For You created my inmost being; you knit me
together in my mother's womb. I praise You because
I am fearfully and wonderfully made.
Psalm 139:13-14

After being married for almost a year, despite our differences and my fear of his fits of rage, we decided it was time to start a family. It didn't take long for me to conceive. We were elated when the pregnancy test came back positive. Another song was born!

Becoming One

(Verse One)
I wonder what God will give me,
a daughter or a son,
My heart is now rejoicing,
For this life that's just begun, this life has just begun.

(Chorus)
The love of two people, the miracle of becoming one,
Becoming one, becoming one, becoming one.

(Verse Two)
I wonder about tomorrow,
and the days I've left behind,
There's so much I want to give to,
This beautiful baby of mine, this beautiful baby of mine

(Verse Three)
I can't wait to feel you move in me,
In the secret place you hide,
I can't wait to hold you in my arms,
And rock you to sleep at night.

I was so excited to be carrying a new life inside of me. I couldn't wait to see the baby protruding from my belly. It seemed to take forever. I didn't even show until the end of my fifth month. During my pregnancy, I continued working at the flower shop. I had been there just long enough to receive the medical insurance that covered the entire pregnancy and hospital expenses. Some of the women there were very protective of the baby. They were afraid to let me go into the flower cooler because they thought the baby would freeze. They never let me step up on a ladder to get the supplies I needed; they always retrieved them for me. The baby seemed to break the language barrier and soften their hearts toward me. Most of them were moms and sensitive to my state of pregnancy. They even gave me a surprise baby shower.

In my second trimester, my sister Jenna and her husband Mark invited Andre and I to a Christian concert. As the singer hit a high note, I felt the baby move inside of me for the first time. When the concert was over, the pastor had an alter call inviting anyone who had a tugging in their heart to come forward and surrender their life to Jesus. I felt something stirring deep inside of me. It was a strong yearning, yet gentle at the same time. I started weeping and told Andre I wanted to go forward. He put his arm out and tried to stop me. He was uncomfortable with my decision, and I was disheartened by his disapproval. Again, he controlled me. I felt the calling of the Holy Spirit but did not respond. I left the concert still longing for peace while Andre commented that the singers were only performing to make money.

The last trimester wasn't easy, especially with Andre's negative comments. I tried not to let his remarks bother me but they still hurt me very deeply. He tried to justify his behavior by telling me I was more emotional and sensitive being pregnant. Actually, I was wounded and scarred from being subjected to his continual abuse. I was physically very healthy but the baby had settled into a breached position. This baby was determined not to turn no matter how many exercises I did to manipulate the movement. It was difficult to breathe with the baby's head high under my rib cage. In my ninth month, my boss decided it would be easier for me to relocate to a smaller shop located in a hotel very close to where I lived. This flower shop was only one mile away from my condo. Almost every day I would walk along the beach to work. Sometimes it seemed like forever to get there. I waddled down the sand like a turtle, but I felt invigorated by the fresh ocean air and it was great exercise. At that time, Andre had taken a job at the same hotel as a chef, which made it convenient for us to go home together.

It was so amazing to me how everyone thought the baby was a boy by the way I was carrying - straight out in front like I had swallowed a basketball. Even strangers would come up to me and tell me I was having a boy. My mother said that was an old wives' tale and total nonsense. She had carried all eight of her children - boys and girls - the same way. She predicted that I was going to have a sweet, baby girl. When we went for a sonogram, the nurse told us she thought it was a girl. Andre wanted a boy so badly that he refused to believe her. As he argued with her, she became increasingly annoyed and commented that she hoped he would love the child no matter what sex it was.

During my pregnancy, I kept a journal recording my innermost thoughts. I also wrote several poems that expressed my deepest emotions; this was one of my favorites:

Longing

Tears fill my eyes as I look at the bed,
Where my baby will soon be laying its head.

I look out the window at the enchanted sea,
The waves are restless like the feelings in me.

Today's my last day before the surgery they plan,
I'll try to be as brave as I can.
I'm amazed and marvel at the wonder of it all,
Can't wait to hold this creature so small.

I'm excited with all the mystery and suspense,
I'm treasuring the whole experience.
It's hard to believe that nine months have passed,
I'm going to see my baby at last.

Because the baby was still in a breech position, a Cesarean delivery was scheduled. When that glorious day finally came, I was fully awake and aware of everything going on but numb from the waist down from an epidural. I felt no pain, only pressure, when the doctor pulled the baby out. It was a pink surprise! Of course we had packed a boy outfit to bring the baby home in, so Andre left the hospital to find something girly for her. He came back with a pink dress that had "Thank Heaven for Little Girls" embroidered on it. It was so precious.

Our baby was so beautiful with her big blue eyes, bright pink lips, and chubby little cheeks. Celia was a precious gift from heaven. Andre's dream came true, Celia was named after that beautiful song he loved and had sung for me so tenderly. He marveled with delight as he held his daughter in his arms for the very first time. I was elated from the miracle of my firstborn. When my mother came to visit me at the hospital, I felt closer to her than ever before. As she doted over Celia and gazed at her little face with love, my heart was overwhelmed with the thought of her giving birth eight times!

As the epidural eventually wore off, the pain was excruciating. I felt like I had been cut in half. *I was!* I was only given low doses of pain medicine because I was nursing. Every time I fed Celia I had to hold her in a "football" position to avoid putting pressure on my abdomen. After five days in the hospital, they told me I was going home. "You've got to be kidding me!" I exclaimed, "I can hardly walk, how I am going to take care of a newborn baby?" I felt so overwhelmed. When we arrived back to our apartment, Andre moved her cradle close to my side of the bed. I cried from the pain of the surgery whenever I had to get up to take care of her.

Andre was so protective, that anyone who wanted to hold her had to wear a sterilized hospital gown. Being a mother for the first time, I also went a little overboard myself. I would always blow dry her hair after a bath, in fear that she would catch a cold.

Celia was so amazing! As she grew, so did my love for her. She was delicate, sweet and incredibly smart. By her first birthday, she was walking and talking. Celia's verbal skills were so advanced that many people didn't believe me when I told them what she could say. They were amazed when they heard her speak and communicate in sentences. I read to her constantly. Every day, we put numerous puzzles together, and sang many songs and lullabies. Sometimes I had to remind myself that she was only a baby because of her level of comprehension. She was a little genius!

Time was flying so fast; the months were slipping away much too quickly. I treasured every moment of being a mother. It was more wonderful than I had ever imagined it would be. Each stage of her life brought new discoveries and exciting adventures. Life was a gift and wonderful through the eyes of a child.

On the other hand, life with her father was not what I had dreamed it would be. When things were going his way, he was content but when they weren't, that spirit of rejection was triggered in him and he became a different person. He was extremely jealous of Celia. He frequently complained that I wasn't paying enough attention to him. From the time we left the hospital, Andre insisted on doing things his way, no matter what advice we were given by the doctors and nurses. I knew that he loved his daughter, but this controlling nature and temperament were alarming and made me even more protective of her.

By this time, Andre had left his job as a chef and acquired his real estate license. After working as a realtor for a while, the housing market took a dive. Andre was stressed out about our financial situation and convinced me that working for a wealthy family would be lucrative for us. I reluctantly agreed. He would be their private chef, while I would perform light housework and help him in the kitchen. So I thought! I ended up being the full-time housekeeper. I cleaned a huge mansion with Celia in a snuggly on my back. It was grueling with only one day off a week. The only part of the job I looked forward to was designing floral bouquets for their extravagant home.

After the drudgery of cleaning all day, I had to assist Andre in the kitchen at night and leave Celia alone in her crib. Sometimes I could hear her crying for me from the bottom of the stairs of our living quarters. That desperate sound ripped my heart into pieces. I was torn between taking care of her, doing my job, and not creating more tension with Andre. Stressed and exhausted, weight melted off of me while the resentment within me grew. Celia must have felt neglected and abandoned. I was stricken with guilt. Arguing about it only caused more havoc and strife. I was so relieved when they decided to let us go. We did make a tremendous amount of money in a short amount of time, but sacrificing my motherly instincts was more than I could bear. Our lives were either feast or famine, financially *and* emotionally.

During the first two years of Celia's life, Andre had several job changes. This became increasingly difficult because of the already rising stress between us. The tension of our financial burdens led him into intense fits of rage. When this happened, it was like an explosion of emotions that were stirring inside of him. The more hardships we faced, the more I became the victim. He continued to blame me for his own failures. Sometimes he acted like a raving lunatic. He would criticize me and he continued to be physically aggressive. He controlled every detail of our lives. Celia and I were so frightened from this hostile environment that I finally tried to set some boundaries for this unacceptable behavior. When these episodes happened, we would escape for a short period of time. We would usually stay with one of my close friends for a few days.

When I felt it was safe to return home, I told him things had to change, but I was still afraid of him. Despite my shredded self-esteem, I still wanted my marriage to work and convinced myself that, this time would be different. My codependency didn't magically disappear and neither did his tirades and narcissism. These attacks were continually damaging to my soul. I felt trampled on. I was in a prison of emotional turmoil. I had never been in a relationship with a man like this before.

At this turbulent time of my life, my mother was in and out of the hospital suffering from congestive heart failure. Doctors did not expect her to live much longer. We only had one car, so I was unable to see her as often as I would have liked. Sometimes my sister would come and pick me up, or I would borrow a friend's car to visit her. On these long rides to see her, I reflected on the many fond memories I had growing up. I loved listening to her write songs on the piano, sitting on her lap while she sewed, and watching her sketch beautiful landscapes. She was an amazing lady!

Even though she suffered greatly with arthritis, she never let her handicap be an excuse. She always persevered. Her artistic talents were very impressive. My mother was extremely outgoing and loved to socialize. I marveled in watching her sing and dance with joy! Sadly, after my father's death, she became very lonely and depressed. Celia's love made her feel alive again. She adored her. She once told me, she didn't have the heart to clean Celia's little fingerprints off of her glass coffee table. She also told me she loved Celia's laugh and wished she could bottle it to cheer her up on rainy days. She was a wonderful mother and grandma, and our hearts ached at the thought of losing her.

On the evening preceding my mother's death, I received a call from one of my sisters. The doctor informed her that our mom was expected to pass away the next day. In a state of panic, I started to prepare to leave that night so I could see her one last time. Andre was working in real estate again, but couldn't earn enough money to support us. We were really struggling because the savings from our job as live-ins was depleted. With no income, he was on edge and at the end of his rope.

I needed the car to go see my mom one last time before she passed away. When I told him this, he sarcastically told me to take a bus. I was appalled by his reply and infuriated with his insensitivity. In my anguish, I told him that I wished I had never married him. Those words made him erupt like a volcano!

He started screaming and cursing at me, then came after me like a violent, raging storm. I ran from him as fast as I could. I desperately tried to escape, but he cornered me at the top of the stairway. I was terrified! I raised my arms to block my face as his fists slammed several blows to my body. I somehow managed to get away quickly enough to lock myself in the office, the room closest to the stairs. He forcefully pounded on the door, demanding that I open it. I stood on other side, bewildered and quivering with fear that he would break the door down or even try to kill me.

When he finally gave up, and I no longer heard the sound of banging fists against the door, he then began shouting at me. He demanded that I finish ironing all the clothes that were draped over the couch in the office. At the horrifying sound of his voice, I fell to the ground and curled up on the floor in a fetal position. My whole body trembled from the shock of his vicious attack and injustice. Through groaning tears, I wrestled with the disbelief that this really happened to me and that my mother was going to die the next day. I was stunned from this cruel and monstrous act of violence. His eccentric behavior had escalated to the point where his once intense love for me had twisted into extreme hate. I felt like I was living with Dr. Jekyll and Mr. Hyde. This betrayal and violation of his vow to "love and protect" was worse than anything he had ever done to me.

I took some clothes from a pile of laundry and used them as a pillow and blanket to cover my aching body. I closed my eyes and tried to sleep, but my body was swelling from where he had hit me. I was in so much pain; I couldn't stop sobbing. I wondered what I was going to do next in this dangerous predicament. With almost no sleep, I called my sister Jenna early in the morning to come and rescue us. She assured me we could live with her as long as we needed to. She was more than concerned for our safety. She told me to grab some clothes, wake up Celia, and wait for her outside. I felt so humiliated.

Unaware of spiritual warfare at the time, I felt a demonic presence in my house. I was still stricken with fear when I cracked open the office door and made my way down the hallway that led to the master bedroom. I slowly turned the door's handle, entered the room, and walked toward my dresser. Andre was waking up, so I changed directions and tiptoed cautiously toward the bathroom. When he turned his head toward me, evil still lurked in his eyes. With a stammering voice, I told him that Jenna was on her way to take Celia and me to the hospital to see my mother. Then, hoping he might be remorseful, I showed him my bruises and said, "Look at what you did to me!" He responded with a devilish laugh and told me that I deserved it. I scrambled to grab some clothes as quickly as I could, scooped Celia out of her bed, and rushed outside to wait for Jenna. I tried to stay calm but it was impossible. I didn't know if Andre would come after us and continue to be violent. As I waited on the front porch for Jenna, I held Celia closely, rocking her back and forth in my arms. She could feel my tension and we both cried. I thanked God that she was sound asleep the night before when this living nightmare took place.

On the way to the hospital to see my mom before she died, Jenna tried to calm me down. Just being in her presence was an oasis for me. She was a godly woman who reflected the love of Jesus. She always went out of her way to help others, especially me when I needed her.

When Jenna and I arrived at the hospital, our other sisters were gathered together in a private room waiting for us. I tried to act as if my only concern was for my mother, but I was still bewildered from my own affliction. I wore long sleeves to cover up the bruises that were evidence of what he had done to me. Only Jenna knew the truth about what had happened.

I was able to spend some time alone with my mom before she died. I told her how much I loved her and how sorry I was for anything I had ever done that hurt her. I could hardly bear seeing her struggle to breathe in my already fragile state. I was not in the room with her when she passed away. I was in a private waiting room with Celia who was fast asleep. Celia had curled up in a chair in the corner of the room like a little kitten taking a nap.

We all had peace knowing that my mother was with the Lord, for she had a personal relationship with Jesus and a steady prayer life. Still, we painfully mourned her passing. Before she died, she told us she did not want a viewing. After her funeral service, she wanted to be cremated and have her ashes placed in a vault beside my father.

Andre was notified about the funeral, but I did not expect him to attend. He surprisingly showed up, but few words were spoken between us. Andre never apologized for what he did to me. Incredibly, he tried to convince me that we needed to come home with him and be together as a family. Everyone was grieving and I was still in a state of shock from all the devastation.

As crazy as it may seem, when the service was over, we actually left with Andre. As we were leaving, Jenna's eyes followed us intently as we walked through the door of the funeral home. I'm sure she was concerned for our safety, but in all of the confusion, we left with him anyway.

He once told me that if I ever tried to take Celia away from him, he would take her out of the country, and I would never see her again. He was not a citizen of the United States, so I took his threat very seriously. The fear of losing my child overpowered my fear of his abusive behavior towards me. I knew it was ludicrous to leave with him, but he still had an eerie control over me. In my state of bewilderment and grief, I didn't want to take the chance of losing my little pink surprise even after what he had done to me. Celia's innocence and love was a treasure I could not afford to lose.

> ***The sweet spirit of a child can bring you
> joy even in turbulence and sorrow.***

CHAPTER 4

A Spiritual Awakening

Jesus Can Transform Your Life.

*I will give you a new heart and put a new spirit in you. I will
remove from you your heart of stone and give you a heart of flesh.
Ezekiel 36:26*

After returning home, I slept in a different room for some time. I tried to
block out all that had happened, but the lingering thoughts of this living
nightmare still affected me. I resumed my daily activities and wished I
could just live a normal, peaceful life. After some time, things cooled
off a bit. I made Andre promise that he would never hurt me again but
there wasn't much sincerity in his voice. Things eventually got better, but
then the cycle started all over again. After another job loss came anger,
withdrawal, and more abusive behavior. Like gravity controlling the ebb
and flow of a raging tsunami - I knew the storm was out there, but didn't
know when or how hard it would hit.

This time it hit hard! His dysfunctional behaviors forced Celia and
me to leave him again. He became suicidal and kept a gun hidden under
the mattress. I was petrified! He came down the stairs looking for me with

the gun in his hand. We fled in such fear that we left barefoot without any belongings. We ran down to the end of the street and frantically knocked on a neighbor's door. An elderly woman answered and allowed me to use her telephone to call Jenna to come rescue us again. We stayed on the neighbor's porch and hid behind the patio furniture until Jenna arrived.

After this incident, we ended up living with Jenna and her husband Mark, who were newlyweds. I felt like we were intruding on their privacy in their one bedroom apartment, but we had nowhere else to go. We slept on their couch for several weeks. Jenna and I were very close. Being the two youngest children of eight, we grew up sharing a room together. She was the type of person that gave to others with a sacrificial love. She would never turn me away.

Shortly after moving in with them, I received an arrangement of a dozen peach roses with a note attached. It didn't say, "I love you" or "I miss you" or even an "I'm sorry." The message on the card was: "Bring my daughter home to me now!" It clearly revealed his controlling nature, and I refused to ride this roller coaster again.

I sought help and counsel from an organization that helps women in distress. They generously gave Celia a toy to keep her busy and even let her keep it. They provided an informative pamphlet advising me to read it very carefully. I already felt rejected, embarrassed and betrayed, yet what I read made me feel even worse. The forms of abuse listed on the pamphlet were unfortunately all too familiar to me.

There was no alcohol or substance abuse, but it was clear to me that Andre was a rage-aholic. My heart wasn't the only thing that had been battered and bruised. I was shocked when I realized I had experienced all of the signs of abuse that were listed. The only thing that differentiated my case was the cycle described on the back of the pamphlet. It showed a cycle of events, explaining how anger would escalate into assault, followed by withdrawal, and finally remorse, with the abuser promising he would never do it again. In my case, Andre was rarely sorry for hurting me.

The counselor told me that according to some statistics, 99 percent of men of this nature do not change even after counseling. Women need to be warned: if a person is abused just one time, it will most likely happen again. The counselor then told me that if I wanted to try to salvage the relationship, I needed to set strict boundaries and seek professional help for both of us.

I had to decide what to do with my life and how I would provide for my little girl if I chose not to go back to him. Andre was still her father and I didn't know how I would survive on my own. He controlled all of the finances. I never had a credit card, never wrote checks, or ever paid a bill. In my first marriage, Don handled the bills, and we usually paid for everything else with cash. I felt very naïve and inexperienced in the basics of life. There was a lot to learn if I were to survive on my own. The fear of it all added to my stress. If I had known the trauma that awaited me with Andre, I would have been cautious and paid more attention to the red flags and warning signs instead of falling for him so fast. I felt desperately insecure coming from a large family, often times feeling lost in the shuffle. I longed for love and attention.

After a time of separation, Andre and I were finally able to communicate on the telephone. He agreed to counseling and to stop the brutal behaviors that were tearing our family apart. Before I returned home, I met with him at a local church where we started counseling sessions. While Andre and I were venting, the woman who was trying to counsel us became perplexed by the seriousness of our issues. She wasn't equipped to hear our disturbing story, or to help us handle it. I was instructed to set boundaries, and Andre was told to promise he would stop the violent and dysfunctional behaviors. We were then told to get professional help. I was expecting some spiritual guidance but the Word of God was never mentioned. She did say a quick prayer at the end of each session, and I was very comforted by that.

My sister Jenna and her husband were Christians and had been praying for us for some time. They also encouraged me to read the Bible. They kept planting seeds as the Lord was preparing my heart for what was to come. After living with my sister and her husband for many weeks, Andre asked me to please return home. He agreed to further counseling and begged me to attend a Bible study he was invited to by an old friend he had bumped into at the grocery store. I remembered visiting Andre's friend and his wife once for a culinary presentation in their home when I was pregnant with Celia. They were a very friendly couple with five children and one on the way. Their house was decorated with Bible verses framed on the walls throughout most of the rooms. There was a peaceful presence in their home that was illuminating. I was hopeful that maybe this time things would change. I wanted to give Mark and Jenna their privacy back. I felt this was a sign that it was time to go.

After Celia and I returned home, we immediately started attending his friend's Bible studies. On one of these enlightening evenings, the truth of the Gospel was shared. I said a special prayer asking Jesus to come into my heart and be the Lord of my life. As I was praying, it felt like a white light was shining down on me from heaven. My heart was overwhelmed with God's peaceful presence. Something incredible happened! Jesus saved my soul. As stated in Acts 4:12, "*Salvation is found in no one else, for there is no other name under heaven given to men by which we must be saved.*" I found out afterward that Andre had prayed that same prayer in another room. I wanted to believe that this was the miracle I was hoping for.

We immediately started attending our friend's church, which was very charismatic. My heart was awakened to praise and worship music, and I continued to feel the supernatural presence of God. It was the manifestation and power of His Holy Spirit.

This church was quite different from the traditional service we had attended growing up. They had a band that played contemporary Christian music while the congregation sang songs giving glory to God. The preacher, who had long hair and a beard, wore jeans and leather cowboy boots. He shared passages from the Bible and taught us how we could apply them in our daily lives. I was developing a personal relationship with God through prayer and reading the Bible. I was falling in love with Jesus, the lover of my soul. He saved me by taking the punishment for my sins and God knows there were many! There was a new life inside of me; I was "born again" and now part of the family of God. I started thanking God for my blessings and asking Him for help in times of need. I read the Bible, but sometimes it was hard for me to understand.

A particular passage in the Bible that helped me better understand what it meant to be born again is presented in John 3:1-7 where Jesus tells the following story.

> "*Now there was man of the Pharisees, named Nicodemus, who was a member of the Jewish ruling council. ² He came to Jesus at night and said, "Rabbi, we know that you are a teacher who has come from God. For no one could perform the miraculous signs you are doing if God were not with him."³ In reply Jesus declared, "I tell you the truth, no one can*

see the kingdom of God unless he is born again." [4] *"How can a man be born when he is old?" Nicodemus asked. "Surely he cannot enter a second time into his mother's womb to be born!"* [5] *Jesus answered, "I tell you the truth, no one can enter the kingdom of God unless he is born of water and the Spirit.* [6] *Flesh gives birth to flesh, but the Spirit gives birth to spirit.* [7] *You should not be surprised at my saying, you must be born again.""*

Although I was a new creature, there were old patterns in our marriage that still needed to change. I hoped that going to church would soften Andre's heart and help our relationship. It seemed to for a while.

At one service in particular, I noticed a young woman who was close to my age. She was raising her hands and praising God with a genuine joy and reverence that I had never seen before. Her name was Amy and it didn't take long before we became friends. People at this church were very enthusiastic about their faith. Some people even danced down the aisles or fell on their knees as they worshipped. The people in the congregation were very loving and always made us feel welcomed, even though the way they behaved in church sometimes appeared to me to be crazy and inappropriate.

I was awakened to the truth that God was alive and real. Jesus was the bridge to heaven, and the Holy Spirit that now dwelt within me, was my comfort and my guide. New melodies started to well up in the depths of my soul. I picked up my guitar again and began writing songs of praise and worship. I soon became involved in the music ministry and flourished as a songwriter. My songs were anointed and I felt blessed to be used by God. I realized that God had protected me from becoming successful in the secular music business. God's plan for using my gifts had prevailed.

Even as a small child, music moved me very deeply, touching my heart of hearts. I would sing my heart out to anyone who would listen. I sang in school talent shows, performed in dramas and musicals, and loved every minute of it! Singing was a catharsis for me. I could get lost in rapturous melodies for hours.

On my sixteenth birthday, my parents bought me an acoustic guitar. I was ecstatic! It wasn't long before I wrote my first song. It was a ballad of love about my high school boyfriend. Songs that followed reflected the pain of a tainted heart. The lyrics of my songs expressed the typical wavering emotions of a young teenage girl. Now that the Lord had taken my music to a place of reverence and glory, I was grateful for this marvelous gift.

The pastor of our church was amazing! He once preached about how being a Christian doesn't mean that your life will be perfect. He quoted a Scripture that really intrigued me as a new believer: *"I have told you these things, so that in me you may have peace. In this world you will have trouble. But take heart! I have overcome the world"* (John 16:33).

Even though our lives were being transformed, the devil was still at work trying to destroy our marriage. There were many strongholds from the past that needed to be broken. The idea and study of spiritual warfare was new to me, but I had already experienced it and was now beginning to understand it. I knew it was real! I learned that there was power by speaking the name of Jesus, and when you did, the demons would flee: *"Therefore God exalted Him to the highest place and gave Him the name that is above every name ..."* (Philippians 2:9).

The old nature of our flesh was still hanging on and Andre became very legalistic. He would often criticize me for not reading the Bible enough but his actions were not aligned with his quotations from the Bible. His love toward me was mostly conditional and it seemed like I was always doing something wrong. I knew that I was not perfect: *"For all have sinned and fallen short of the glory of God, and are justified freely by his grace through the redemption that came by Christ Jesus"* (Romans 3:23-24).

I still wanted to try to make our marriage work. I tried to be a subservient wife and helpmate but it wasn't easy with his verbal attacks and abuse. He was still trying to control me. These cycles persisted and hurt me very deeply. God's design for a husband is to love and protect his wife, not to harm her. I prayed that things would change and asked God to help me forgive Andre. I harbored a root of bitterness and was still afraid of him. I tried not to dwell on all the negative things I had suffered through in our relationship. I took comfort in reading a passage from His Holy Word: *"Finally, brothers, whatever is true, whatever is noble, whatever is right, whatever is pure, whatever is lovely, whatever is admirable – if anything is excellent or praiseworthy – think about such things"* (Philippians 4:8).

We sought help from different Christian marriage counselors who advised us directly from the Word of God, but hearing it and applying it seemed like two different things. We started going to a new church where I soon became involved in the music ministry again. We learned more about spiritual warfare and the curse of the generations. These studies were intriguing to me because I knew there was truth in it. There were demonic forces that continued to destroy my family. We were still struggling immensely in our relationship. There were many strongholds that needed to be torn down.

One evening when I entered Celia's room to kiss her good night, I saw her kneeling by her bed praying. She was asking God to please make her mom and dad stop fighting. My heart was breaking for her as I wrote this song:

Miracles Can Happen

(Verse One)
Walking by I heard her cry and I saw her on her knees,
I heard her whisper softly asking Jesus please,
Let mom and dad be happy, please don't let them fight,
Her little heart was breaking, and she touched my heart that night.

(Verse Two)
So I said a special prayer
For the Lord to teach me how to care,
Through all the years, through all the pain,
I built a wall so high,
Lord please help me break it down,
Fill my home with a peaceful sound,
Though sometimes I don't know why,
I'll give it one more try.

(Chorus)
Miracles can happen, I need one right now,
We can be a family, Lord please show us how,
Miracles can happen, I believe it's true,
We can be in harmony, there's nothing God can't do.

(Verse Three)
Daddy where you going, are you coming back home,
Mommy looks so sad, she's feeling so alone,
I don't really understand, why it is this way,
Maybe you can help us, please hear the words I pray.

A miracle is exactly what we needed. At church, we appeared to be this wonderful couple with a beautiful little daughter by our side, but behind the scenes, there was a deep dark secret. I kept it hidden; I was too afraid and embarrassed to reveal all the ugly details, even to Christian counselors. In one counseling session I attended alone, I was told that if my husband had ever hit me, the police would have to be notified. That frightened me even more. I imagined that if I called the police, Andre's anger would escalate against me.

I had convinced myself that for the most part, things were better. His abuse was now mostly emotional. Sometimes after a display of anger, he wouldn't talk to me for days, acting as if I didn't exist. It was baffling when I couldn't figure out exactly what I did that caused him to withdraw from me.

One Saturday, a friend from our church invited Andre to a Messianic synagogue. He came home with such zeal about what he experienced that he was about to explode. He explained to me that Jews and Gentiles attending this service were born-again believers. They were worshipping Yeshua (Jesus in Hebrew) together in one accord. They danced in a circle singing Hebrew songs praising Adonai (God in Hebrew). Andre was adamant about me going to see this for myself.

When I went to this messianic temple for the first time, I was puzzled at what I saw. These people were even more charismatic than the people in the churches we had previously attended. We continued going to our church on Sunday and the temple on Saturdays. We started to learn about the Jewish roots of our Messiah and how the Torah and the New Testament were connected and of equal importance. Yeshua is the promised Messiah to the Jewish people. God is the vine and we are the branches. Jewish believers represent the natural branches and the Gentile believers are grafted into the vine, collectively forming one body of believers. These Jewish believers considered themselves "completed Jews." Their eyes were opened to the truth that the scriptures reveal in Isaiah 53:5: "*But he was pierced for our transgressions, he was crushed for inequities; the punishment that brought us peace was upon him, and by his wounds we are healed.*" It was all so exciting but still very new to me.

One Saturday at the Oneg (lunch) after the service, the Rabbi approached me. Andre had told him that I sang and played guitar. The Rabbi told me he had been praying for someone like me to come to the congregation to lead worship there. I laughed under my breath. I told him that I wasn't Jewish, didn't speak Hebrew, and was definitely not an accomplished guitarist! That didn't seem to matter to him. He believed I was the answer to his prayer. He told me to pray about it to see if the Holy Spirit was leading me into this calling. Soon after, the woman who led the dance ministry started teaching me Hebrew praise and worship songs. In God's appointed time, I became the worship leader for this Messianic Synagogue. Only by the grace of God and the power of His Holy Spirit, was I able to achieve this challenge.

I was inspired by this dynamic form of worship and wrote several messianic songs with the Rabbi. His sensitivity to the moving of the Holy Spirit in the service was amazing. I knew God had brought us to this place for a purpose. The Rabbi and his wife were also professional psychologists, so when the turbulence returned, we started marriage counseling with them. Again, I was afraid to reveal the dirty details of the physical abuse. They were already appalled at some of the things we shared with them.

Andre soon became jealous of the Rabbi and more possessive of me. He also felt threatened by my new position of leadership. Even though there was more friction between us, I knew this was my calling to lead worship, and I continued to grow in the Lord. Celia even prayed to ask Jesus into her heart and was already witnessing to children on the playground! The Lord was evidently working in our lives but the enemy was still on the warpath.

Be aware of spiritual warfare … it is real!

CHAPTER 5

The Power of a Child's Prayer

Believe in the Power of Prayer.

Therefore I tell you, whatever you ask for in prayer,
believe that you have received it, and it will be yours.
Mark 12:24

By this time, Celia was six years old and longing for a little sister. She started praying that God would give her one to play with and to love. I adored children but was very concerned about bringing another child into this dysfunctional family. So far, I had been successful in preventing that from happening by using different birth control methods, which Andre and I both agreed upon. Soon after Celia's prayers and petitions, I knew I was pregnant.

It was a time of famine for us. Andre had lost another job. We now lived even further from my family and I missed them terribly. How I wished I lived closer to my sisters to help me through these trying times.

Every time we received the phone bill, Andre became angry with me for calling them. I feared going to the mailbox that the bill might be there!

To confirm that I was pregnant, I went to a Crisis Pregnancy Center because the test was free. I already knew I was pregnant but when I got the results, I held my stomach and grieved in agony over this child. I feared for what this baby might have to face. I cried so much; it was like a life had ended instead of rejoicing for one that was just beginning. When I returned home, I gave Celia the news that God had answered her prayers. Despite how I felt, she was elated! Even though I would carry this baby for nine months, I believed this child was God's gift to her.

During my second pregnancy, my emotions were tossed around like a ship sailing on a restless sea. I tried to be happy and loved being pregnant, but the instability of my marriage and Andre's abusive behaviors weighed heavily upon my mind. There was turmoil deep inside of me and I was concerned that the baby could feel it too.

When the sonogram revealed that the baby was a girl, Andre was disappointed again that he wasn't going to have a son. He later made the remark that God must want him to have daughters. Celia on the other hand, jumped for joy with exuberance! She looked forward to sharing a bedroom with her baby sister, who would sleep in the crib that was once hers. We envisioned the baby in little pink dresses with ruffles and lace. We couldn't wait to put booties on her tiny feet, like a living baby doll. We were blessed with an abundance of clothes that were passed down from a friend's twin girls. One day Celia and I put them all on little carousel hangers and hung them up in the closet. The baby's wardrobe left little room for Celia's dresses. I wondered how this baby would ever have the chance to wear all these beautiful clothes. I also had been blessed with three baby showers from family, church, and friends. God was so faithful in providing all that this baby would need and beyond.

At the end of my pregnancy, I was baptized at the beach one glorious afternoon. As I was submerged into the water, my belly was popping up like a buoy. It was a memorable event in more ways than one. We celebrated by going out to dinner to a restaurant that had a sensational view of the ocean. It was a beautiful evening and I felt the joy of the Lord.

Suddenly, a storm came our way that rocked my boat and pushed me over the edge. It came at a time of feasting, but famine was not far from the table. Even though I was in my last stage of pregnancy, I was working part time as a floral designer and also as a musical entertainer at daycare centers. My income paid for Celia's tuition at a private Christian school. During this time, Andre lost a very good paying job – again! He had been working as a chef at a private country club. Things seemed to be going well, but they decided to terminate him. I was in my last trimester and we had no savings. With a baby on the way and my employment soon coming to a close, I was at the end of my rope. This time, I was the one who became angry, withdrawn and depressed. Andre tried to isolate me, which abusers often do to their victims, which made me feel even worse.

When he had lost jobs in the past, I tried to encourage him that he would find a better one, but this time, I was totally exasperated. The pattern repeated itself too many times and the arguing escalated. By this time, we were two months behind in rent with little money to live on for food and necessities. The time for the baby to be born was quickly approaching. We had taken a refresher Lamaze class to prepare for the birth of our second child. After one of these classes, Andre became angry and pushed me outside against the car, arguing with me that I did not perform the breathing technique properly. I was so mortified and fearful of his explosion. I knew the baby inside of me could feel my anxiety.

After one week past my due date, I was admitted into the hospital to be induced. On the way there, we dropped Celia off at my friend Amy's house. This dear friend that I had met at church was always a blessing to my children and me. Celia and Amy's four-year old daughter Abby were like sisters. Amy was more than happy to have Celia come over and give her a break from playing Barbie dolls. Amy also had a three-month-old son named Elijah. We were both pregnant with our second child at the same time, which made us develop an even stronger bond. Amy was a joy and had an engaging personality. With a sweet giving spirit, she genuinely cared about others. *"For God loves a cheerful giver"* (2 Corinthians 9:7).

Amy and I shared many common interests, mostly our love for the arts. We worked on several art projects together and enjoyed these endeavors immensely. We often laughed at the blond things we did and sometimes competed to see who did the blondest thing that week. All of our stories could fill a book. We used to laugh about what we could name it, *"How Blond Can You Be?"* or *"God Loves You and He Loves Blonds Too"*!

We had a very special friendship. I knew I could confide in her. She was the only person besides Jenna who knew about all of the abuse. Amy was a prayer warrior, and was always there for me in body and spirit. Praying for this baby to come out quickly was now at the top of her prayer list. I was also hoping and praying for a quick delivery. We were trying for a "V-BAC," which is an abbreviation for vaginal birth after cesarean. I did not want to experience the aftermath of surgery again!

After checking into the hospital room, I nervously anticipated this birth. After I was induced, the contractions became more intense. I tried to be the hero Andre wanted and insisted that I be. I resisted an epidural and tried using Lamaze breathing techniques to get me through the pain. The nurse was very kind and empathetic. As she saw me suffer, she reinforced that it was my decision if I wanted an epidural. Then she stated that my husband was not the one who was giving birth! When the contractions became more intense, I used a bookmarker with a picture of Jesus in the clouds as my focal point. I later found out this particular picture comes with a poem called, *"Safely Home,"* which reflects the beauty of heaven.

After pushing for more than an hour, this baby did not want to come out. Finally, my doctor, who was six months pregnant, forced the baby out by using a suction instrument. The doctor's assistant stood on the bed straddling over me, pressing on my abdomen to push the baby out! We were all determined to deliver this baby without requiring another C-section surgery.

When the baby's head finally appeared, the doctor asked me if I wanted to touch it. I remember screaming, "No! Just get it out!" It was a horrible birth experience. I was in excruciating pain as she was traumatically forced out of my womb. I was in another zone when they laid her on my breast to nurse for the first time. I tried to focus on this miracle of life, but the pain was overwhelming.

After her birth, she didn't scream or cry like most babies do. Instead, she made a whimpering noise, as if she was humming a soft melody. Even the nurse commented that she sounded like she was singing. I told the nurse that she probably was. I had been a worship leader for my entire pregnancy, with a guitar resting on my belly. I'm sure she could hear the music and feel the vibrations. She was a new light in our lives so we named her Leena, which means shining light.

After Leena's birth, Amy brought Celia to the hospital to meet her new baby sister. I will never forget the love and tenderness in Celia's eyes when she saw Leena and held her for the first time. Even Andre and I shared a moment of bliss as we watched Celia stroke Leena's hair and sing to her, "Jesus loves me, this I know ..." Through tears of joy and pain, I silently prayed for the Lord's protection and hoped things would be different for her. Andre was still unemployed and times were tough. I was afraid we would not be able to pay our rent again, and that we might get evicted. We didn't even have enough money for food or diapers. I felt that Andre had failed me in so many ways and took all of his frustrations out on me.

When Leena was only a few weeks old, we left the synagogue and started going to a new church. I was reluctant to leave but Andre insisted because of his conflicts with the Rabbi. I was so sad to leave my friends and congregation. I mourned this loss, and felt that Andre was ripping me away from the ones I cared about and loved. He was threatened by my connection to other people and jealous of those relationships.

The transition to the new church was better than I had expected. Some of the women there reached out to me and I already felt loved by them. One woman in particular, knew our desperate situation and shared our financial needs with the pastor. When we attended the next service, the pastor called us by our names to come forward. We were baffled as we slowly walked up to the stage. He proceeded to explain our financial burdens to the congregation. In his compassion, he asked that if anyone felt led by the Lord to help our family, to come forward and give a love offering.

As we stood there, people began to leave their seats and come down the isles. The elders were standing on each side of us holding baskets. I couldn't believe the mass of people that came forward. The baskets were soon overflowing! One generous man came forward and told the pastor that he would personally match the total amount of money given. We wept and were humbled by this incredible miracle of God's faithfulness and provision. We left the church that day with the amount of money we needed to pay the back rent and to sustain us for the next few weeks. I was relieved and filled with hope believing God was still there for us. Leena was in my arms as this miracle took place. I thought about how some day I would share with her this testimony of God's unfailing love.

As Leena grew, she must have thought she had two moms. Celia took such good care of her. She would dress her, sing to her, rock her, and even stroll her around in a baby doll carriage. The only thing she could not do was nurse her! Instead, she would nurse her baby doll while I nursed Leena. I loved seeing them together and marveled at the bond between them that was growing stronger every day. We nicknamed Leena "Spunky doodles" because she was so bubbly. She truly lived up to her name. She was a shining light in our lives. She was so joyful and had a sweet tender spirit. I loved to watch her dance around with her white blankie, which was a special blanket she was attached to and could not live without. At nine months, she started saying several words and it wasn't long before she could say sentences like, "Momma, I love you." Those words were a gift to me, and I will treasure them forever. Her verbal skills were beyond her age. She undoubtedly was following in Celia's footsteps.

God hears the plea of a child longing for love.
God's faithfulness comes in many forms.

CHAPTER 6

No Turning Back

When You're at the End of Your Rope, Let Go and God Will Catch You.

Trust in the Lord with all your heart, and lean not on your own understanding; in all your ways acknowledge him, and he will make your paths straight.
Proverbs 3:5-6

Around the time of Leena's first birthday, my marriage had reached the point of total hopelessness. I became numb from Andre's controlling and abusive behavior. I was so fragile. I displayed random outbursts of raging tears just to release my bottled up emotions. I even felt like I lost my identity. Nothing I did was ever good enough for Andre. I felt so worthless and depleted. It was in the autumn when it all came to an end. I knew there was no turning back.

Andre was playing too rough with Celia and physically hurt her, leaving a bruise on her arm. I cautiously intervened in her defense, but Andre became increasingly angry at my attempt. He started cursing and downplayed the seriousness of his actions; manipulating us into thinking we were to blame. The argument escalated into a treacherous violent rage.

I was mortified! I prayed for God to surround us with angels to protect us as I had done many times in the past. I nervously shouted at Celia to get Leena and run away as fast as she could. Andre had the devil in his eyes as he came after me, screaming that he was going to kill me.

I ran into the kitchen, frantically grabbed the phone off the wall, and called 911 in fear of my life! I yelled to the operator – "He is trying to kill me!" Andre grabbed my hair with one hand, trying to hold me still while he aimed his other fist at my face. I dropped the phone, quickly ducked down, and managed to get away. Andre had tripped over a kitchen chair, which allowed me just enough time to escape his wrath. I then locked myself in the bathroom by the girls' bedroom.

Celia had run into the bedroom with Leena and they were hiding behind the clothes in their closet. Sadly, this had become a familiar hiding place for them when they were frightened by the sound of us fighting. As they clung to each other, silent tears froze upon their fearful little faces.

In a very short time, I heard the sound of police knocking at the front door. As Andre reluctantly let them in, I could hear him trying to convince the officers that everything was fine. Obviously it was not, there was no hiding the evidence. In his rage, he had violently broken the children's bookshelf - books were scattered all over the floor.

While Andre was talking to the police, I came out of the bathroom and hurried into the girls' bedroom. I opened their closet door and tried to coax them to come out, reassuring them it was now safe. I pulled them toward me and held them both in my arms. We clung to each other and cried uncontrollably.

One of the police officers came into the room and asked me if Andre had tried to hurt us. I could no longer conceal the truth of the terror in our lives. The officer then walked over to the window to close the verticals. He spoke softly, explaining that he wanted to protect the children from having an awful memory etched in their minds, the vision of their father being handcuffed and taken away. Just before the verticals were closed, I caught a glimpse of Andre with his head held down in shame.

As the officer walked back toward us, I noticed a small angel pin attached to the collar of his uniform. He spoke with a calm voice and tried to console us. He suggested I call someone to help me figure out what I should do next. I knew this time we would never return to the turbulent environment that we had tolerated far too long. It was the end of a grueling chapter of my life - I wish I could have burned all the ugly pages.

Shortly after this traumatic scene, the phone rang. It was Judy, one of my dearest friends. I could no longer hide the truth from her. After I shared all that had happened, she immediately came over. She came with her daughter who was a couple years younger than Celia. Our little girls played in a room together as she helped me pack my car with everything we could possibly fit in it. I was an emotional wreck, but she was very calm. She told me that when her mother left her father, they didn't have time to take any of their belongings. She didn't want this to happen to me! Judy told me that if I didn't take everything I wanted now, I would probably never see these things again. She was a Godsend.

As we loaded the car with clothes, baby albums and belongings, I treasured her friendship even more. We hugged and cried, and before we said our final good-byes, I quickly ran back into the house to make one final check.

Suddenly the phone rang – it was Andre. The sound of his voice was alarming! He demanded that I bring some medicine to the jail that he had been taking for high blood pressure. As ironic as it may seem, after he wanted to kill me, I actually tried to get the medicine to him the next day. He still had a strange control over me. When I made this attempt, the police would not accept it. I was disgusted as I watched them drop the medicine into the trash after all my efforts.

After that alarming call from Andre, I went back outside to thank Judy and say goodbye. We hugged and cried knowing it was the end of a chapter, but also knowing there was still a rough road ahead of me. I drove away from my home knowing I would never want to return there after all that had happened. My mind was flooded with so many uncertainties. I wondered where and how we were going to survive. Knowing I needed the support of my sisters, Amy encouraged me to move to the town where they lived. Jenna, who now had a two-year old son named Joshua, was five months pregnant. She and her husband lovingly agreed to let us live with them until I could make it on my own. Praise God! As devastated as I was, I felt like an imprisoned bird that was released from her cage. I was relieved to know that I would never live that way again.

With a restraining order, domestic violence case, and visitation issues to face, I was still overwhelmed and numbed with fear of the unknown.

It all seemed so complicated. Thankfully, I could count on my sisters for help. I held on to Jesus with every fiber of my being. I prayed for direction and the peace of God's presence. I knew the Holy Spirit would guide me and God would provide for all of our needs.

When we had first arrived at Jenna's house, there was a card lying in the grass by her front door. It had a Bible verse on it that said, *"And my God will meet all of your needs according to his glorious riches in Christ Jesus" (Philippians 4:19)*. I knew it was not a coincidence and this message was for me. Jenna's home would provide a safe haven for us. Her living room was converted into a playroom with colorful Disney décor. It was wonderful and whimsical. My girls had so much freedom and fun living there. It was also a blessing to us that another one of my sisters, Audrey, lived right down the street.

That September, there was a new public school opening in the neighborhood, just a few blocks away. Celia was accustomed to attending a Christian school, but I could no longer afford the tuition. I was financially destitute, so I had no choice but to enroll her in a public school.

Every day, Leena would go with me to bring Celia (or "sissy" as she called her) to school and then to pick her up at the end of the day. In the mornings, they could hardly part from each other, hugging and kissing countless times before saying good-bye. At pick-up time, they were always excited to see each other again. As for me, my mind was troubled with so many unanswered questions. How would I support myself? Who would care for my children while I worked? I wondered if Andre would come after us and take revenge for leaving him or even try to kidnap the girls. All these tribulations were leading up to the worst event and misery that was yet to come. This family of four, which had just become three, was about to become two.

Sometimes life is unbearable, but we must
trust in God's ultimate plan.
We may not know what our future holds, but
we do know that God holds our future.

47

CHAPTER 7

My Darkest Days

In Your Darkest Days, His Light Can Still Shine Through.

The Lord is my light and my salvation - whom shall I fear? The
Lord is the stronghold of my life – of whom shall I be afraid?
Psalm 27:1

It was October 6, 1986, and we had been living with Jenna and her family for exactly two months. The period of time for the restraining order had ended. Early that afternoon, Andre came to pick up Celia for his allowed visitation time for the weekend. I was still nursing Leena, who was almost a year and a half old, so it was a great excuse to keep her with me. When I walked Celia out to say good-bye, Leena was in my arms. They reached for each other and hugged so tightly, I didn't think they would ever let go! My heart was torn. They embraced each other with so much love before they were separated and said their final good-bye. Leena was distant and withdrawn from Andre, but as he drove away she started waving good-bye.

Jenna and Mark were busy packing up the family car for a short trip. Before they left, I held Leena up to the car window and she wrapped her arms around Jenna's neck. They tenderly hugged good-bye, and then I opened the door to the back seat so Leena could give her cousin Joshua a kiss. He had become her playmate and her best friend. He called her "baby Leena" and she called him "boy". She loved to chase him around the house trying to kiss him. He would eventually let her catch him and then reciprocate the kiss. Little did we know that their good-byes would be their last until they would see each other again in heaven.

My sisters adored my girls. Earlier that week, Jenna and I were waiting in the garage for one of our older sisters, Karissa, to come over for a visit. It started raining, so Leena and Joshua splashed in the puddles as they anticipated her arrival. Karissa always brought our children delicious sweets. This time it was powdered donuts. Karissa was tender hearted and very nurturing, our little ones could feel her love. Once, Leena even said I love you to her. She offered to help watch my children while I went back to work to support them. I was grateful for that.

Karissa told me an endearing story she was blessed to have witnessed while she taking care of Joshua and Leena one day. I had gone on a job interview at a florist and needed her. While Joshua was playing with Leena, he fell down and started crying. She lovingly wrapped her security blanket around him and gave him a big hug. She had such a sweet, tender spirit. Little did we know how precious all those moments and memories would become.

The first night Jenna was gone on her trip, Leena and I slept together in her queen size bed. We were both restless and woke up several times. When we woke up the next morning, I dressed Leena in a pretty black and white checkered dress that had big colored buttons. It looked so adorable on her. It was actually a shirt that Celia used to wear. When I sat Leena down between my legs to put her little black shoes on, she said, "twos" instead of shoes and we both giggled.

There are certain memories that will be forever engraved in my mind. One in particular is of Leena running down the hallway of Jenna's house towards me with open arms waiting for me to scoop her up and embrace her after I had been gone, job hunting most of the day. My most treasured memory is of Leena and Celia sleeping together, cuddled in each other's arms the night before Andre came to pick up Celia.

After Lena and I were dressed for the day and ready to go, we headed off to visit my friend Kira who had two small children of her own. We met at a McDonald's for lunch which had a small exterior playground. Leena loved playing in the balls and tried to pull me in with her, even though it was designed for toddlers. To this day, I wish I had climbed in with her anyway. For many years after this day, I couldn't bear to even drive near that McDonald's location.

As we pulled into Kira's driveway, it started raining. Before getting out of the car, I placed Leena's special white blanket over her head to protect her from getting wet. I held her close to me as I ran to the front door. I will never forget the warmth of her little body so close to mine. The feeling of her head resting on my shoulder at that moment was a precious gift that God gave me - a special frozen moment in time.

After we arrived at Kira's home, we talked for a while as the children played together. Kira then put her children down for a nap and I nursed Leena to sleep in our usual fashion. Just before she dozed off, she looked up at me with her big brown eyes and I told her I loved her. As she lay sleeping on my breast like an angel in my arms, I thanked God for this precious gift. Later, I reluctantly laid her down on a mattress in the bedroom to finish her nap with the other children.

After all the children woke up, we sat them at the dining room table for a snack. They ate cheese slices and apple wedges. This was Leena's first experience in eating an apple so I was a little hesitant in giving her the apple slices. Shortly after she held one in her hand, she took a bite and started to cry as if experiencing some level of pain. I picked her up out of the booster chair, but she began to cry more intensely, as if she was having a tantrum. With the apple wedge still in her hand, I slowly took a bite of it myself trying to distract her from screaming and crying.

She squirmed and pushed away from me so I sat her down on the rug beneath my feet, but she struggled even more. She began rolling on her stomach and arching her back, so I quickly picked her up again. I tried to figure out what was wrong and patted her on the back. It never occurred to me that she was choking because she was still breathing and crying - until she gasped her last breath. Her head then collapsed on my shoulder, her little arms enveloped my neck, and her entire body became limp. A dead silence filled the room. I screamed that she was not breathing and Kira reacted immediately. Thankfully, Kira had just completed a CPR course and knew exactly what to do. She laid Leena's body facing downward over her arm and administered quick blows to her back, but there was no response and nothing came out of her mouth.

She then carefully laid Leena down on the rug and started the CPR process. By this time, Leena's whole body was turning blue and I started to panic. Kira abruptly but calmly told me to dial 911. The operator asked me the address of our location, but I didn't know it. Everything was happening like a whirlwind yet time seemed to be frozen in this fury. It was October 7, 1986 at exactly 5:45PM when the phone call was made.

Kira quickly took the phone from me while still pressing on Leena's chest, gave the operator the address, and briefly told her what happened. As she was on the phone, I placed my hand on Leena's heart hoping to feel something, but there was no movement from her chest at all! I desperately refused to believe what was happening, but at that moment, I knew she was already gone. I started to scream and frantically pace the living room floor. Kira's two small children began feeding off my emotions and also started to panic.

The police responded quickly by arriving only a few minutes after the emergency call, but it seemed like an eternity to me. There were two officers; one coaxed the children and me into the bedroom while the other officer, Rob, tried to revive her. When I was in the other room, I desperately and repeatedly prayed, "Lord, please breathe life into her." When Rob entered the room, I asked him if she was breathing. His only reply was to just keep praying. He even knelt down and prayed with us while the other officer was with Leena. Before he left the room, he told us that he had a young daughter of his own.

Over the next few minutes, he went back and forth between Leena and me. I kept asking him if her heart was beating. He avoided answering the question initially. But to give me some sense of hope, he finally told me there was a faint heartbeat. At this point, my body became numb and I started to tremble. I was going into shock as time seemed to stand still.

I then heard the sound of a siren coming down the street towards Kira's house. I dashed out the front door just as the paramedics arrived. I grabbed one of them by the chest and started screaming, "My baby is not breathing!" His rescue crew proceeded to enter the house and pushed all the living room furniture against the walls to create space for their life-saving equipment.

As Leena's limp blue body lay on the floor, I watched them as they cut her little dress open down the middle with a pair of scissors. They placed a tube down her throat and attempted to remove any obstruction from her airway. Officer Rob then quickly led me back to the bedroom to protect me from seeing their invasive attempts to save her life. The house was filled with pandemonium and chaos. The paramedics placed a defibrillator on her chest in another attempt to save her. I could hear these shock treatments from the bedroom, so I came running out to see what was happening. It was frightening to hear and see the device on her little body.

Rob had followed me to where Leena and the paramedics were. He then told me they were going to take her to a nearby hospital emergency room. Rob asked me if I wanted to ride with him in the police car. Observing my continuing state of paranoia and confusion, the paramedics never asked me if I wanted to ride in the ambulance with Leena.

I left with Rob and we followed closely behind the emergency vehicle. For many years, the piercing sound of sirens triggered a state of panic within me. On the ride to the hospital, I desperately wanted to cling to Rob's hand for comfort and strength. But I didn't dare. Just being with him made me feel more secure and protected. He showed compassion in the way he was taking care of me.

As we pulled up to the hospital emergency entrance behind the ambulance, I saw the paramedics lower the stretcher with Leena's little body lying on it. It seemed so out of proportion. We followed them through the hospital doors, and Rob and I were directed to a private waiting area. Kira and her husband were the first to join us. She began calling my sisters and other family members and told them to come to the hospital as quickly as possible. An admittance nurse requested Leena's insurance information, so I gave her the medical card I recently acquired from Medicare.

I realized I needed to contact Andre. When I reached him on the phone, I told him Leena was not breathing and that he needed to come to the hospital immediately. His hostile reply shattered my soul when he screamed, "What did you do to her?" I was so petrified from his voice that I literally threw the phone through the nurse's reception desk window.

When I returned to the waiting room, my body began shaking relentlessly and my skin tone turned ashen – a pale white. Rob kindly covered me with some hospital blankets and brought me some water. He offered to stay with me as long as I needed him, even though by this time he was already off duty. His compassion was exactly what I needed at that moment and I knew God's hand was upon me even in the midst of this tragedy.

When my other family members arrived, we were still trying to reach Jenna. She was seven months pregnant with her second child and I believe the Lord protected her from this awful day of despair. Thankfully, we were able to reach the pastor and worship leader of the church we had been attending. Other members of the congregation arrived some time later.

Still covered with blankets and in shock, I remember a doctor coming into the private waiting room where we anxiously waited for an update on my baby Leena. The doctor, completely exhausted, collapsed into the corner chair with a defeated sigh of frustration. He questioned me about my family medical history, and then shared the news that is a mother's worst nightmare – my daughter had passed away. His face looked distraught, trying to comprehend the fact that he was unable to revive her. He told me he worked on her for a long time and didn't understand why he couldn't bring her back to life. He looked baffled. I can still visualize the disappointment on his face.

Shortly after that, two men wearing suits led me to another room and began asking me questions. Unknowingly, it was really an interrogation because the cause of death was still not determined. I was devastated! The x-rays and tests did not yet reveal any information to explain her sudden death. Finally, weeks later, when the autopsy report was released, the cause of death was officially determined. It stated: "asphyxia by food, aspirated by apple," and "manner of death: accidental"

Prior to this fatal accident, Leena had briefly stopped breathing on three different occasions. I shared this with her pediatrician at periodic check-ups, but he was not alarmed and stated that she was in good health, attributing the incidents to freak accidents. I have always wondered if there was something more seriously wrong with her that the doctor had overlooked.

After I had been interrogated, we returned to the waiting room where my family was mourning Leena's death. A nurse came in and asked if we wanted to see her. As difficult as it was, we slowly made our way down a long hallway where she was being kept in a separate room. Unable to stand, my sisters' arms supported me as we walked together. Each passing step that brought me closer to her lifeless body was more painful than the one before. As we entered the room, Leena laid there in a big hospital bed wearing only a diaper. There was a small tube coming out of the side of her mouth, held in place by a piece of tape.

She looked so beautiful and peaceful. By this time, my crying had turned into a constant moaning. The nurse gently sat me down in a chair next to Leena and asked me if I wanted to hold her. She then lovingly and carefully placed her in the cradle of my arms. As I rocked her back and forth, I spoke to her as if she were still alive, saying, "It's okay, mommy is here now." My family gathered around me and we all began praying the Lord's Prayer. I froze in one position, holding her close to my heart. After many moments of silence and sorrow, the nurse asked me if I was ready to give Leena back to her. I shook my head indicating "no.". After allowing me these final moments with her, she tenderly lifted Leena out of my arms and I staggered back down the long hallway with the help of my sisters.

By this time, Andre and Celia had arrived. Andre was pacing nervously in the private waiting room while Celia was in a state of bewilderment. One of the officers at the scene of the accident was standing outside the emergency entrance when they arrived. Without even knowing who they were, he spoke to them, saying, "I'm sorry, but your daughter did not make it." This still remains a mystery to me that he would share this terrible news without knowing who they were for certain. Officer Rob asked me if I needed him any longer before leaving the hospital. As he left, one of my sisters overheard him saying that he didn't know if he could continue working in the police force after this devastating experience.

Back in the private waiting room, Kira slowly knelt down to make eye contact with Celia and told her that her sister's spirit had gone to heaven. She didn't seem to grasp what was happening. At the tender age of seven, she already suffered grievously from being torn between the affection of her mother and father. She probably blocked it out in disbelief or didn't understand that her sister had really died.

A nurse entered the waiting room and asked if we wanted to see Leena together as a family. Another nurse pulled Andre and me aside, advising us not to let Celia see her, concerned that the vision of her lifeless body would haunt her memory for years to come. We agreed that it was not in Celia's best interest to view Leena's body at this point. Celia begged us to see her, but we wanted to protect her.

I barely made my way down that long hallway again with only Andre accompanying me this time. Leena had been moved to another room around the corner and was lying in a hospital baby crib. She still looked so peaceful but I was disturbed that her diaper appeared to be soiled. I told the nurse that we needed to change her, still feeling my motherly instincts to nurture and care for her. Andre stroked her fine soft hair and as he wept over her little body, his tears dripped down onto her bare chest. He spoke softly to her saying, "Good-bye, my little love, you are with the Lord now."

When we made our way back to the lobby, my family, music minister and members from our church were waiting for us. We held hands in a circle and prayed for peace, comfort, and strength for the days to come. Andre reluctantly joined the prayer circle, stating that nothing more could be done. Someone in the group quoted the Scripture from Psalm 46:1: "*God is our refuge and strength, an ever-present help in trouble.*" I desperately longed to be with my sister Jenna. She was a source of strength and peace for me, but we were still unable to reach her.

It was late in the evening and Andre insisted that Celia drive with him from the hospital to Jenna's house. I didn't want her to be alone with him so I drove back with him also. Andre stayed there that night in the room that we had been living in for two months. Before the end of the night, I attempted to console Andre, hoping that he might comfort me in return after losing our child, but his heart was cold and non-responsive. He spent a long time on the phone that night speaking to a woman that I later found out was his girlfriend. He had always been flirtatious with other women, but I never thought he would ever cheat on me because he was so possessive and always wanted me with him. After I left him, he obviously pursued a relationship with another woman.

I desperately kept trying to reach Jenna and my best friend Amy, who was also out of town. When I was finally able to contact Amy, who knew my children better than anyone in my family, I shared all of the traumatizing events with her. She was devastated and assured me that she would come to my rescue as soon as she returned home from her trip. Amy prayed for me before hanging up, but I was inconsolable.

Shortly after that phone conversation, my sister Audrey, who lived down the street, came over to Jenna's house to stay with me for the night. She tenderly held my hand and was a comfort to me, but we were too deeply disturbed to sleep. The phone rang around 2:00 AM. It was Jenna. She finally received my daunting messages. I told her what happened to Leena and that she was now with the Lord. Jenna later conveyed to me that the conversation seemed so surreal; she struggled to grasp the reality of it. I pleaded with her to return as quickly as possible. Her husband and two-year old son Joshua were still sleeping so she told me they would leave first thing in the morning. After hanging up, Jenna told Mark that Leena had died. In their distress, they were unable to go back to sleep, so they packed their things immediately and drove back home during the middle of the night. Jenna told me she wept the entire trip home as Joshua slept in his car seat.

The next morning, Andre woke up early and left. I was glad but wallowed in the harsh reality of the day of despair I was about to face. Without any sleep, I was very weary but when I finally heard the sound of Jenna's car pull into the driveway, I dashed out the door as fast as I could. As we held each other in anguish, we tried to capture a moment of solace, but the pain was much too deep.

One of my older sisters that lived out of town came as quickly as she could, arriving later that day. I was always very close to her. She once told me that whenever I would appear in her dreams, I was always a little child. I was so glad to see her, feel her embrace, and share tears of comfort and sorrow. I have fond memories of her and my other older sisters nurturing me as I was growing up. I needed them more than ever now.

There is no greater pain for a mother than to experience the death of her child. Being a Christian does not exclude you from suffering in this life, but God will carry you through it.

CHAPTER 8

Letting Go

There Can't Be A Shadow Without Light.

Even though I walk through the valley of the shadow
of death, I will fear no evil, for you are with me;
your rod and your staff, they comfort me.
Psalm 23:4

On that mournful day after Leena's death, some of my sisters began removing her belongings from the room we had been sleeping in. They thought I would become even more distraught by having her things in view. When I saw them doing this, I became very upset and agitated. I wanted to keep all of her belongings with me, mostly her treasured white blanket. I told them not to wash it or remove her scent that permeated it; a scent that I didn't ever want to forget. It remained in that blanket for many years, allowing me to savor her memory.

Because of my state of devastation, my sisters began arranging for the funeral and burial without my involvement. They later consulted with me about the details. We decided that the stone on her grave would read, "A child of God, A precious daughter, Celia's little sister." There was a special section in the cemetery called Babyland where the graves were covered with toys and stuffed animals, which was heart-wrenching to see. Unfortunately, no burial plots were available there, so we had to bury little Leena in an adult grave.

We all agreed it was best to bury her under a palm tree, close to the area where the vault of our father and mother's ashes were kept. Celia was extremely upset that her sister would not be buried with all of the other babies. We tried to explain to her that this was the best spot and eventually her body would decay and turn back to dust. Her soul would be with God forever, and she would be waiting for us in heaven. Being only seven years old, Celia initially thought she could keep Leena's body and play with it like a baby doll. It was very disturbing to hear her make that confusing but hopeful remark. For days, Jenna's little boy Joshua would roam the house looking for Leena. It was heart breaking to hear him call her name continuously, but she was nowhere to be found.

During the next few days, Celia became bewildered as family and friends came to visit us and showered her with gifts. These tokens given with heartfelt intentions actually made her feel more confused. She spent time alone in another room as we tried to shelter her from the conversations about the burial preparations. She didn't understand what was happening and felt neglected. She was given a special princess Barbie doll from a relative, a doll she dreamed of having for several months, but nothing seemed to make her happy. Her world had been shattered and my emotional stability was shaken to its core. I was unable to eat or sleep.

Not only was I an emotional wreck, my body kept physically producing breast milk to feed a baby that was no longer alive. I had to wrap my chest with ice packs to relieve the pain and swelling. Sometimes, I had grieving attacks that caused my entire body to shake while I screamed and cried uncontrollably. During these episodes, Jenna would lay her hands on me praying and calling upon the name of Jesus. She also quoted many Bible verses, which brought life to my empty existence. When the peace of the Holy Spirit came upon me, my body would relax and my crying subsided. The Lord's awesome presence was so strong and evident that it transformed my deep pain into the peace that surpassed any human understanding. God was alive in my life and still revealing Himself to me, even in my darkest days. Knowing Leena would be waiting for me in heaven, I was comforted by the verse in 2 Samuel 12:23 when King David's baby had died, *"But now that he is dead, why should I fast? Can I bring him back again? I will go to him, but he will not return to me."*

The funeral and closure I had to face in the days to come were more than I thought I could bear. My entire being was frozen in a prison of pain. Being in a state of shock felt like I was in a glass enclosure of solitary confinement. I observed the world around me, but nothing could touch me because my pain had already reached its peak. In a way, it is God's gracious shield of protection.

In Jenna's continuing generosity, she took Celia and me shopping to buy us something to wear for the funeral. I was so weak when I tried on clothes that I almost fainted in the dressing room. I remember lying on the floor while Jenna fed me crackers to give me some strength. While we were in the store, I felt as if I was watching a video of the world around me. I was removed from the reality of events, as the rest of the world kept revolving. I stood in the shadow of my own existence.

After this happened, Jenna was able to get a prescription for a mild sedative to calm me down when I needed it, and to help me sleep at night. This medicine also enabled me to survive the viewing and burial services. Jenna and Mark's constant kindness amazed me. Not only had they provided for my girls and me, they paid for the entire funeral. Andre was unemployed, again.

The dates for the funeral services were delayed, giving Andre's family time to travel in from overseas. Meanwhile, Jenna was preparing to make the ceremony as painless as possible. She bought two beautiful white embroidered baby blankets and had the idea of draping them under Leena's body and over the casket. This would form the illusion of a basinet and soften the scene if we decided to have an open casket.

On our long drive to the viewing, Jenna read Bible passages out loud to us. I stared out the car window, gazing up at the clouds in the sky. I wondered where heaven was and why my little girl was taken there so early in her life. Leena was gone and so was a part of me. My little Celia sat quietly with us in the back seat. How heart breaking that her sister was gone and her mother's heart and mind were so far away. I was distantly removed in a state of shock, grief and post-traumatic stress. I tried to explain to her what was happening, but I could hardly grasp it myself. Jenna tried to comfort us by reading a scripture from 2 Corinthians 5:1-9:

> *"For we know that if the earthly tent we live in is destroyed, we have a building from God, an eternal house in heaven, not built by human hands. ² Meanwhile we groan, longing to be clothed instead with our heavenly dwelling, ³ because when we are clothed, we will not be found naked. ⁴ For while we are in this tent, we groan and are burdened, because we do not wish to be unclothed but to be clothed instead with our heavenly dwelling, so that what is mortal may be swallowed up by life. ⁵ Now the one who has fashioned us for this very purpose is God, who has given us the Spirit as a deposit, guaranteeing what is to come. ⁶ Therefore we are always confident and know that as long as we are at home in the body we are away from the Lord. ⁷ For we live by faith, not by sight. ⁸ We are confident, I say, and would prefer to be away from the body and at home with the Lord. ⁹ So we make it our goal to please him, whether we are at home in the body or away from it."*

When we arrived at the funeral home for the viewing, six days after her death, I could barely walk through the doorway into the room where her body lay. We weren't sure if we should have the casket open for viewing. Jenna slowly approached the coffin and assured me that she looked very peaceful. The funeral director lifted Leena's little body as Jenna placed the beautiful white blankets under her and over the white wooden coffin. He commented that this was a great idea and would suggest it to other families who had lost a baby.

He gently placed Leena's body on what now appeared to be a baby basinet. Celia and I had chosen a green floral print dress for Leena to wear, one that Celia had worn for Easter when she was a toddler. On Leena, the dress went all the way down to her little white shoes, which were embroidered with pink flowers across the top. It upset me that her body just barely fit into the coffin. I told Jenna I was concerned about Leena because she didn't look comfortable. She tried to assure me that Leena was safe and cozy wrapped in Jesus' arms, her body was only her temporary dwelling, and we would see her again in heaven.

Leena had a messianic Jewish funeral. As I predicted, Andre and I had a huge conflict over who would perform the ceremony. Hundreds of people came from different churches and messianic synagogues that we had attended, along with family and friends. The funeral ceremony was beautiful, with numerous Scripture verses and poetry being read. One verse that was a great comfort to me was: "*in my father's house are many rooms; if it were not so, I would have told you. I am going there to prepare a place for you*" *(John 14:2)*.

Andre and I didn't sit together at the funeral. No words were exchanged between us, not even a momentary glance. Many people were not even aware that we were separated. Some children from Celia's first grade class attended the funeral, which really surprised me. One of my friends told me not to be alarmed if I saw something strange in Leena's casket. Her little boy had made Leena a necklace out of rope and beads, and wanted to place it in the coffin with her so that she would look pretty in heaven. This little boy knew Leena well because I used to take care of him while his mother worked. This really touched my heart and made me cry even more.

By the end of the funeral, I was so completely numb that I could not even cry anymore. I was exhausted from greeting and consoling all the guests, trying to reassure them that Leena was in heaven. When it came time to leave, I knelt down by Leena's coffin and Celia approached me. She peeked into the heavenly bassinet and started touching Leena's body, examining her very closely. She told me she wanted to keep the little doll that was cradled in Leena's arms. She didn't understand when I told her it was her baby sister's favorite doll and that I wanted her to be buried with it. She became angry with me, insisting that I give it to her! I told her I would give her another one of Leena's dolls.

I then put my finger in Leena's little hand and didn't want to let go. It felt like she was holding on to it as if she was alive. I will never forget that feeling. I held on to her white blanket throughout the service. In a way, it became my security blanket. I only parted with it for a few moments, asking Amy to hold it for me. She knew that blanket all too well. She had taken care of Leena numerous times and said it was an honor to hold it at her service, even for a short while.

When the room had cleared out, my family remained with me. They allowed me all the time I needed in those final moments with Leena. Jenna told me that I should say a special prayer giving Leena back to God. We prayed that special prayer together, but in my heart, I could not let her go. No words could describe what I felt at that moment. I was so weak and fragile. I knew that only the power of the Holy Spirit could sustain me. I took comfort in the words from 2 Corinthians 12:9:

> *"But he said to me, my grace is sufficient for you, for my power is made perfect in weakness. Therefore I will boast all the more gladly about my weaknesses, so that Christ's power may rest on me."*

The rest of the night was a blur of disbelief. We woke up early the next morning for the burial service. As we approached the cemetery, many people were already there. They were seated in chairs on the grass facing the little white coffin. Tears began to flood my eyes. As I opened the car door, my knees buckled from beneath me and I almost collapsed. My sisters came running to help me while Jenna ran to a nearby fountain for water. She quickly placed a pill in my mouth to calm me down, and I frantically tried to swallow it. We slowly made our way over to the chairs and sat directly in front of the casket. This time, it looked like a cold hard rectangular box, too harsh to be containing my sweet little Leena.

There was a cold stillness in the air. A stone wall between Andre and me. Scriptures and poetry were read as we all wept and wallowed in disbelief. Near the end of the burial service, suddenly, a cool breeze began to blow. It encircled us all. My dear friend Nina, leaned towards me and whispered, "It's the Holy Spirit – do you feel God's presence?" I felt God's presence and the peace of the Ruach (the Hebrew word for wind, referring to the Holy Spirit). *"The wind blows wherever it pleases. You hear its sound, but you cannot tell where it comes from or where it is going. So it is with everyone born of the spirit" (John 3:8).* Through showers of tears, I burst forth singing Amazing Grace, and everyone joined me in a rhapsody of praise. *"You are my hiding place; you will protect me from trouble and surround me with songs of deliverance" (Psalm 32:7).*

Shortly after, I pulled some pink roses out from one of the funeral arrangements and handed them to Officer Rob to bring home to his wife and little daughter. I graciously thanked him for trying to save Leena's life and for all he had done for me. I was also very grateful for my friend Kira's love and all her efforts to revive Lena. She always had a sweet spirit. After going through severe hardships in her own life, she was a blessing to others and especially to me on that fateful day. She managed to stay calm through it all and knew exactly what to do. If this had happened when I was alone, the guilt of not knowing how to revive Leena would have haunted me forever. It could have been so much worse.

I always felt a special connection to Kira, especially at this time of my life. I never blamed her; I knew she did everything in her power to save her. The number of our days is in God's hands. God was in control even in the midst of tragedy and sorrow, providing the right people at just the right time. Kira later told me that there was a peace in her home - as if angels had been there. This gave me a beautiful vision of angels coming and gently carrying Leena up to heaven. As devastating as it was, I knew this had to be her time to go. As it says in Psalm 139:16: *"...your eyes saw my unformed body. All the days ordained for me were written in your book before one of them came to be."*

After the burial, family and close friends met at Jenna's house to share a meal that our church had prepared for us. After we arrived, Andre kept insisting that Celia go home with him. He tried to convince me that it was the right thing to do. He wanted her to spend time with his relatives who had traveled from abroad and rarely had the opportunity to see her. Celia did not want to go and clung to me. I couldn't bear the thought of not having her with me after all we had been through; we needed each other. I knew she would be better off with me than with him. His family was always kind and loving, but Celia hardly knew them.

I still felt controlled and manipulated by Andre. I was so distraught and emotionally drained that in a state of confusion, I reluctantly let her go. She started to cry when I told her we needed to pack some of her clothes to go with her father for a few days. That was a decision Celia and I both regretted.

The very next day, while speaking with Celia on the phone, I found out Andre's girlfriend was living with him. I became infuriated and demanded he bring Celia back to me immediately. Being subjected to that situation would only bring her more confusion. She was already devastated from losing her sister and all that had happened. I was so upset that I had allowed her to go with him. He did bring her back to me that evening. We had just walked through the valley of death, we needed comfort and to feel the peace of God's presence, not more conflict and confusion.

> **It is never easy to say good-bye. Yet even in the valley of the shadow of death, it is possible to feel God's presence.**

CHAPTER 9

Striving to Survive

Persevere through the Pain; Learn to Dance in the Rain.

I know what it is to be in need, and I know what it is to have plenty. I have learned the secret of being content in any and every situation, whether well fed or hungry, whether living in plenty or in want.
Philippians 4:12

At the time we experienced this tragic loss, Celia had just started second grade. A new public school had just opened down the street from Jenna's house. Celia ended up missing two weeks of school after Leena died, but because she was advanced academically, this did not affect her grades. Emotionally though, she was withdrawn, keeping all of the pain she felt hidden inside of her. When she returned to school after Leena's death, I walked her down the hall to her classroom each morning. It was terribly sad remembering how Leena used to hug and kiss Celia good-bye at the door. This memory of them together was painful and bittersweet.

I had read that the things in life that cause the most stress were death, divorce, moving, changing schools, and changing jobs. Sadly, we were experiencing all of these at the same time. Yet, through all the hardships, God was faithful. We felt His presence with us through our struggles and He continued to provide for all of our needs.

There was a counselor at Celia's school who was also a Sunday school teacher. The Lord had placed it on her heart to start two support groups for children: one for divorce victims and another for children experiencing a death in the family. This woman was clearly sent from the Lord, as both of these programs helped Celia cope and express some of her feelings. She gave Celia a special stuffed animal to sleep with at night, and me a notepad to write messages of love to put in Celia's lunch box. My heart was so imprisoned with pain that it was hard for me to focus on connecting with Celia. Consequently, Celia became attached to this nurturing woman. I went to get help from a Christian counselor and was told that I suffered from post-traumatic stress disorder, also known as PTSD. It is a disorder that develops in some people who have seen or lived through a shocking or dangerous event. Despite all the problems we had, God was watching over Celia by sending her this angel on earth.

At Christmas time, Jenna and I attended a church event that was being held in a Victorian tearoom and gift shop. When we entered the shop, I saw an angelic white dress that would have fit Leena perfectly. As we sat down for tea, I started to cry as the shop owner approached me. I shared my loss with her and how much I admired the little white dress. She told me that Leena was sitting with the angels wearing the most beautiful white dress I could ever imagine. I was so comforted by her consoling words and the love of Jesus that was shining in her eyes.

Shortly after that event, Kira and I joined a Bible study for spiritual and emotional support. It was no coincidence that the lesson was on helping someone cope with the loss of a loved one. We didn't even know the topic of the study before we attended the first session. I was able to give my input on what was most comforting to me while suffering from the loss of my child. Many people just ignored me and kept their distance. They were afraid to talk about Leena, in fear of triggering the deep emotional pain that lay dormant inside of me. This behavior only made me feel worse, as if my child never even existed. I was comforted the most by those who acknowledged her life and communicated their sorrow for Celia and me. I felt a strong connection to those who had also lost a child and shared the same depth of pain.

Many friends kept sending me cards and notes of love and encouragement, especially Amy. These were so comforting and made me feel that Leena's life mattered. I started reading biblically based books about heaven, which reinforced my faith. I received other Christian books from loved ones, which helped me also.

Some people told me to take time to grieve, while others encouraged me to go to work right away to keep my mind busy. Even though the void inside of me was so vast, and it was hard for me to simply function on a daily basis. I found a part-time job at a nearby florist, but I still had grieving attacks. It was hard to cope with customers, particularly those ordering funeral arrangements. The florist soon moved to a distant location, but it was time for me to leave this shop anyway. The wounds were still so fresh.

I found what helped me the most was staying in prayer, reading Scriptures, and talking with other women who had suffered the death of a child. They were the only individuals that could truly relate to what I was experiencing. I went to a support group periodically and was comforted there, but sometimes it became too depressing. In one of these meetings, a woman warned the group not to forget about our children who were still living. Talking about Leena was healing for me, but Celia became angry and withdrawn when I did, and referred to herself as "the other child." She even began to hate Leena. I was unconsciously doing what I was warned not to do.

I was an emotional mess with all the turmoil that still awaited me. Before any divorce proceedings, I wanted to meet with Andre one last time for counseling at a church we had attended in the past. At this time, a woman was still living with him that he claimed he was going to marry. Andre showed up with a large notebook in his hand. He had written a detailed analysis of all that I had done wrong in our relationship. By the end of the session, both counselors agreed the marriage we had was destructive and irreconcilable.

I was so afraid of Andre's behavior, I didn't want Celia to be alone with him. When I went to the courthouse in the county where Jenna lived, I spoke with a woman who was very kind and comforting. She assured me that the law in that county would protect Celia with supervised visitation. Yet after reading the police report, she regretfully informed me that she could no longer be of any assistance. This case needed to be handled in a different county where the arrest took place. She looked very distraught and spoke with compassion, hoping that justice would prevail and Celia would be protected.

A few days later, I went to the courthouse in the county where I previously lived and was appointed a lawyer that would provide services at no charge. That was a great relief to me considering I had no money. The lawyer explained that this service was provided for women who were pursuing a divorce from a husband arrested for domestic violence. I still wanted Celia to have supervised visitation but was warned that if I pursued this, Celia would probably have to take the stand and give testimony of the abuse. This would have been very traumatizing, especially after all she had already been through. I agreed it would be best to work out a visitation schedule with our lawyers, hoping she would spend as little time with him as possible. I couldn't handle any more stress in my state of mind and would never put Celia in that predicament. She was already confused about her loyalty between her father and me. After the restraining order was lifted, Celia had been spending every other weekend with Andre.

When the time came for the hearing, my friend Judy was there with me for moral support. She held my hand in the courtroom as Andre denied the charges, claiming he was not guilty. The judge saw the trepidation on my face and noticed that I was trembling. He stated that it was obvious I was fearful of my husband. He warned Andre that if this case went back to court and he was found guilty, the judge would take great satisfaction in putting him away for at least five years. Judy and I left the courtroom hoping and praying that Andre would come to his senses and admit the truth. His denial would be detrimental to everyone involved, mostly himself.

Andre was given thirty days to restate his plea. He waited until the last day to admit he was guilty. The judge ordered Andre to take an intense domestic violence course; however, he did not order supervised visitation. I was devastated!

After Leena's death, Celia and I continued going to the church we had attended with Jenna and her family. Our church friends were very supportive through all of these trials and prayed for us continually. The first Sunday after Leena died, I sang *Amazing Grace* at the end of the service. There wasn't a dry eye in the entire congregation.

After that service, a young man approached me. He told me that he felt sorry for me and couldn't understand how I could sing and praise God after the death of my child. I'm sure it was the power and anointing of the Holy Spirit that sang through me. *"The Lord is my strength and my song; he has become my salvation" (Psalm 118:14).*

I was still in shock as Jenna walked me down the aisle of the church toward the stage to sing. Even though it was healing for me to sing praises through my pain, my heart was still paralyzed and I felt extremely lonely. I desperately longed for love and companionship, the comfort of a man to hold me and make the pain go away. Consequently, I started dating this man I had met at church. My last memories of Leena were in Jenna's house, so it was painful for me to be there. I went out with this man as often as I could just to change my environment, and try to escape the flashbacks I had of Leena. The most difficult time of coping with the grief was in the quiet and stillness of the night.

I recall a sad moment for Celia one evening as I walked out to this man's car. She came running after me and begged me not to go. This terrible memory is still engraved in her mind. Consumed by my own misery, I hugged her, then told her I needed to go. I just left her there in the driveway as Jenna came outside to get her. She cried feverishly for me to come back. How I wish I could turn back the hands of time and cradle her in my arms. She felt so abandoned. I was so empty that I didn't have much to give. She suffered greatly because of my withdrawal from her and from reality.

I praised God for my sister Jenna and my other sisters who helped me take care of her. Celia was also blessed to have a best friend from school that lived down the street. They hung out together a lot. They helped each other with homework, rode bikes, and played dress up among many other girly things.

Around this time, Jenna's second child Caleb was born. It was very difficult for me to bond with him after losing my own child, but it was healing for Celia to have a little baby to love. Soon after his birth, I wrote the following poem.

Little Baby Caleb

Little baby Caleb, when I look at you,
I see a precious gift, then my heart breaks in two.

For not long ago, a treasured gift was mine,
But now she is in heaven, and I am left behind.

I want to hold and cuddle you,
So quickly you will grow,

But my eyes fill with tears,
For the child I no longer know.

Little baby Caleb, your life has just begun,
While my little baby's life, on this earth is done.

So if I may seem distant, this feeling will occur,
I may be holding you, but my heart is holding her.

I still suffered periodically with grieving attacks. On one occasion at the grocery store, I grabbed a cart and envisioned putting Leena in the toddler seat in front. I quickly released the cart, started to panic, and searched for a pay phone. I was frazzled. Thankfully, I was able to reach a friend from church who came to my rescue and took me out for coffee. She was full of compassion, and I was grateful for her friendship. She came to rescue me several times.

I still existed in somewhat of a state of shock after many months. When the panic and grieving attacks came, I had chest pains and shortness of breath. I had become very skinny. I still had a loss of appetite, and I took long walks to help relieve the stress. One day as I was walking, I started to come out of this catatonic existence and back into reality. While looking up at the sky and my surroundings, my mind and body felt as if I was slowly fading back into a picture of reality. It was a strange feeling that I will never forget.

Shortly after that experience, the male companion I had been spending time with began showing his true colors, and I began to see the light! Not only had he tried to pressure me into having a sexual relationship, he was not a follower of Jesus Christ and did not worship the one true God. This relationship soon came to an end. After this episode, a new opportunity came into my life, a part-time job as a car saleswoman. I was willing to try anything to prepare for my future as a single mom; I couldn't live with Jenna and Mark forever. A relative had given me the chance to work for him at a car dealership, but I still could hardly function in the workforce. It was also embarrassing when customers were telling me specific details of cars, as if I was the buyer and they were the sales person. They obviously knew more about cars than I did! Selling cars was definitely not my forte. I was an artist, not a business-minded woman, but I gave it a try. Soon after I took this job, Celia and I moved out of Jenna's house. We had lived with her for almost a year.

We ended up renting a house with an old family friend named Nina. She was like another sister to me. She was Jenna's best friend in elementary school, and our older brothers were best friends in middle and high school. She also was a single parent. She had a little boy named Jake whom Celia loved and treated like a brother. After a few months in our new home, I lost my job selling cars by not reaching my sales quota. Regardless, God was faithful again in providing for my needs. As I searched for a new job, money and checks would mysteriously appear in my mailbox. Once, I even found a $100 bill tucked in the front seat of my car. I was amazed at these signs of God's provision and it gave me hope. I trusted in His unfailing love. Even though I was barely able to meet our financial needs on a day-to-day basis, God had bigger plans.

Nina was great to live with as a roommate. We were extremely compatible, particularly because we were both clean freaks and kept our house in immaculate order. We both hated to cook because we didn't want to mess up the kitchen. Jenna's husband Mark once asked us if children really did live with us because it was always so clean.

Nina was also a Christian and knew of a young pastor who wanted to start a new church. This church actually ended up starting in our home and branched out into many other small groups. Sometimes, I led worship for the services, which I really enjoyed, but the fellowship from the women was the biggest blessing to me. The children had Sunday school out on the porch and the adults took turns teaching. The church grew quickly and eventually began holding services in a nearby school.

God provided a new job for me at a local craft store, and I soon became manager of the silk floral department. Besides God's faithfulness in providing this job, He placed many people in my path that had also lost children. We ministered hope to each other and were comforted by this special bond. I never read my Bible as much as I did in that first year after Leena's death. I constantly witnessed to others about the Lord and the hope of heaven.

My grieving attacks had lessened but were triggered occasionally, especially when I saw a baby that resembled Leena. I would discretely follow her around and try to imagine that my baby was still alive. I would even browse at little girl's clothes in stores as if I was shopping for her at the age she would have been. One of my sisters told me she did the same thing. In my anguish, I tried to grasp the light of her, but she was intangible. It was still difficult to sleep at night, with flashbacks flooding my memory. In the mornings, the sting of death awakened me with a deep aching in the depths of my soul.

On my first Mother's Day without Leena, Jenna gave me the awesome gift of a video she had put together in remembrance of Leena's precious life. As I watched it, I relished the moments she was here, but other times I couldn't bear to watch it at all. Even photos could trigger convulsions of pain. Sometimes I hung them on every wall and other times I would quickly put them out of sight. Every Mother's Day, her memory comes alive and digs deep into my heart. I saved many of her special things and placed them in a floral paisley trunk. Her little shoes, socks, toys and clothes are reminders of her time on this earth. Included in these treasures were sentimental memoirs and cards from her life and funeral service. Many trinkets were buried in this beautiful trunk; despairingly, a piece of my heart was buried with her body.

On the first anniversary of Leena's death, we held a special service at the gravesite to honor and remember her. I wore white to signify her eternal life in heaven. Some of my sisters and extended family members came to attend this ceremony and also wore white. My dearest friends, Amy and Judy, were there to support me. Officer Rob even came to show his respect. He was the policeman who first arrived on the scene to try to save Leena. To my surprise, he told me he periodically visited her grave. Our music minister showed up on a Harley to perform the ceremony. I sang a few songs with my guitar, ending the memorial with everyone singing "Amazing Grace" like we did at the end of her funeral. It was an emotional and somber event.

When it was over, we all went back to the house that Nina and I were renting. As we ate lunch together, we discussed and pondered the mystery of what it must be like for Leena to be living in heaven. My heart was breaking for Celia. She was very withdrawn and never wanted to go to the grave. She claimed that Leena wasn't there, so what was the point of going. I tried to explain that I wanted to honor her and keep her memory alive. Celia didn't understand and still felt invisible and unimportant. My sisters and I loved on her, but it was not enough after all she had suffered and been through.

I wrote the following poems about Celia and Leena approximately one year after her death.

Leena

Sometimes I can hardly believe this has happened,
The precious little girl who needed all my care,
Lay still without the breath of life,
As I placed my hand on her tender body,
I felt no heartbeat,
It was a frozen moment in time,
A picture of pain and helplessness,
One year later as I try to separate,
The treasured memories from the pain,
God whispers to my fragile heart,
She is still there in the depths of a sacred place,
When I look up to the heavens so blue,
The mystery consumes me,
But it brings heaven,
A little closer to this earth.

Celia

If I could stop the world and step out of time,
I would reach out and take your little hand in mine.
In a field of dandelions, we'd run barefoot and free,
Laughing out loud, just you and me.
But life is a rush and moments fly,
You are growing up and the days slip by.
There is work to do and bills to pay,
And tears to cry for yesterday.

Don't get lost in the mystery of time.
Capture the moments and hold
them close to your heart.

CHAPTER 10

A Soul in Search of Intimacy

God Created Us for Companionship, but Jesus Is the Lover of Our Soul.

*Not only so, but we also rejoice in our sufferings, because
we know that suffering produces perseverance; perseverance,
character; and character, hope. And hope does not
disappoint us, because God has poured out his love into
our hearts by the Holy Spirit, whom he has given us.*
Romans 5:3-5

Tears of Rain

Can your Son shine through my tears of rain?
Will tomorrow forget yesterday's pain?
Can a broken heart ever mend?
Will I find the strength to love again?

As time passed, the anguish and loneliness I felt for companionship was more than my mortal flesh could bear. I loved the Lord with all my heart and soul. He filled that void deep within me and gave me peace, but I still longed for human love and an intimate connection. My life was full of so much loss. I was extremely insecure, feeling the need to always have a man by my side. I felt isolated in my own depth of despair. I desperately wanted to be held by human arms, and told that things were going to get better. I knew God's grace was sufficient for me, yet I still wanted a healthy, loving relationship with a man.

I was extremely lonely, and became impatient. Besides experiencing so much loss, I had insecurity issues and patterns from my past. There was a history of always having a man by my side. I was determined to stay sexually pure this time, committed to walk in the Spirit and not in the flesh. I needed to be very careful and pray for discernment; I didn't want to be taken advantage of in my already vulnerable state. God knew my weaknesses and my heart's desires. *"Watch and pray so that you will not fall into temptation. The Spirit is willing, but the body is weak"* (Matthew 26:41).

My emotions led me to write the following song.

Fleshly Fire

(Verse One)
What is this life You have for me?
Where does this road lead to?
I want to walk along that narrow path,
I want to follow after You, follow after You.

(Chorus)
Don't stand too close to the fleshly fire,
You might fall in and get burned,
When you feel the heat of your own desire,
Take your heart and turn
To the Father's love.

(Verse Two)
It's a lonely game I can't seem to win,
And the clock is ticking fast,
I want a man I can hold on to,
I want a love that will last, a love that will last.

After a few months passed, I was on a quest for companionship. I contacted an old acquaintance that I had met years ago at the church where I became born again. Lance was an incredible guitarist and had periodically led worship there. He was currently the lead guitarist for a Christian rock band and invited me to one of his concerts. Being a songwriter myself, I envisioned us starting a band of our own called *Skies of Blue*. I was very impressed with him; his original songs were amazing and his music intrigued me.

In the beginning, my attraction to him was mostly on an artistic level. He was a bit younger than I and still in the process of completing his college education. He was a gentle soul, extremely introverted, compassionate, and non-judgmental. His personality type was what I needed at this point in my life - he was a free spirit like me and very laid back. There was a calmness about him that gave me peace. His eyes were as blue as the sky, revealing a mysterious depth that drew me to him.

By this time, my divorce settlement was finalized, and I needed to pick up the rest of my belongings from Andre's house. Lance offered to help me. It was an awkward situation because he also knew Andre from our old church. While moving my things amid much tension and animosity, Lance tried to keep peace. Though it was an uncomfortable situation, Lance handled it well. He showed me a different kind of strength; one that was quiet and Christ-like, completely opposite of Andre's forceful, abusive nature.

Lance and I soon began seeing each other more often. We both were night owls, so we spent long evening hours just talking. I didn't know where this relationship was going, but I thanked God for putting him in my life anyway. He comforted me through the continual grieving and panic attacks that gripped me from time to time.

Celia became very attached to Lance. He really devoted himself to her. They spent a lot of time together reading books, having deep conversations, and playing board games. He was extremely tall and strong, and Celia loved when he carried her around on his shoulders! They developed a special bond and were almost inseparable.

During this time, while I was dating Lance, the house Nina and I were renting was being put up for sale. We were grateful to have lived there. It served its purpose for us, and for the Lord. The church that had started in our home when we first moved in together was flourishing. We made wonderful memories there with our children and with many of the church members.

I felt like it was time to venture out on my own, so I rented my first apartment. I did have a bank account and wrote checks at this point in my life, so I wasn't totally clueless! I still felt overwhelmed with being on my own for the first time, so Jenna helped me create a budget.

The complex Celia and I moved into had a lovely courtyard. Our apartment was upstairs, which made us feel safe. We were happy there, and I enjoyed decorating our new home. Celia's room was blue with a splash of bright colored sunflowers, and mine was mauve with mint green accents, which were popular colors in those days.

Lance helped us with this transition, but I was still stressed about handling all of the finances by myself. Even with a budget, I knew it wouldn't be easy, but I still had faith that God would take care of us. I had always been frugal and creative enough to decorate on a dime. My mother used to tell me that I could make something beautiful out of nothing. Her encouraging words remained with me and were put to the test.

I ended up dating Lance for almost two years, but I knew that something was missing. I prayed for God to show me if there was a future for us. The Lord's answer became clear to me through a Scripture in Ecclesiastes where it says to everything there is a season and a time for every purpose under heaven. In my spirit, I felt that Lance's purpose in my life was for a season, which would soon come to an end. He was my soul's companion for that time in my life but was never meant to be my husband. God knew what I needed and now it was time to move on. Lance was a man of God and it was hard to turn the page, but I was still in search of a relationship that would last. I longed for a godly man to share my life with.

Celia had already faced great loss in her life and was devastated when Lance and I broke up. She became angry with me and grieved over my decision. Lance had occasionally been reading a book by C.S. Lewis to her at night, but they never finished it together. He was disturbed by her grief, so he recorded the rest of the book on cassette for her. Celia tried to listen to the recording, but cried at the sound of his voice, and refused to continue the story. I also grieved the loss of this relationship, but God was preparing my heart for another man of God who would eventually end up sweeping me off my feet. God knew the desires of my heart. I knew if I remained faithful to the Lord and put Him first in my life, He would fulfill my deepest longings.

"But seek first his kingdom and his righteousness and all these things will be given to you as well. Therefore do not worry about tomorrow, for tomorrow will worry about itself. Each day has enough trouble of its own" (Matthew 6:33-34).

After Lance and I broke up, I left my job at a local craft store to work at an upscale florist in another town. My boss at the flower shop was a Christian and became like a brother to me. He was a talented designer and a great person. His compassion for people moved me and I enjoyed working for him. After working there for some time, the commute was getting to me. I lost a lot of precious time with Celia, and my car was wearing out quickly, costing me in repairs. My boss didn't want me to leave, and even offered to help me lease another vehicle. I told him, if he gave me his Porshe, I would stay! After the expression of shock wore off his face, we both cracked up. It was hard to leave, but I knew it was the right thing to do.

I began searching for a job that would pay me what I had been making. The Lord opened the door to a florist closer to the apartment where Celia and I were living. When I went there for an interview, the owner Rick stated that he had just hired a designer. He said he would keep my resume on file for future consideration. I told him I would be praying about this job and leave it in God's hands. I still wanted to work there and left feeling hopeful. A few days later, Rick called me and explained that the designer he hired decided to work only part time. If I was still interested, I would need to come in for a second interview. I told him I was a single mom and needed a full-time job to support my child but was interested in hearing what he had to offer. Rick was a dynamic businessman and seemed like a great person to work for.

I had a strong feeling in my heart that God had a purpose for me at this flower shop. Rick still did not need me full time but was able to provide enough hours for me to make ends meet. There wasn't any alimony coming in and only minimal child support. God provided for my needs on a daily basis.

The other designers were really sweet and friendly, making it an easy transition for me to join the team. They were sensitive to what I had gone through and very encouraging. We became close friends over time and bonded together as a little florist family. All of the women were gifted and we admired each other's talents. Each woman had a distinct beauty of her own. I was nicknamed the "Tropical Queen" and became the main exotic floral designer. We worked hard during the holidays but that didn't stop us from having fun together.

There was never a dull moment while working for Rick. He was a strong leader but also a blast of energy! We had barbeques outside the back of the shop, and really enjoyed being together. We even created and celebrated our own crazy holidays (like Bring Your Dog to Work Day), or whatever wild idea we could think of. His personality was so vibrant and engaging that customers would come in to consult with him about their personal problems. He used to joke around that he should charge them by the hour. It was the best job I ever had and it was about to get better.

Rick told me about a guy from his church that he wanted me to meet. He thought that we would make a good couple. He also told this guy, he had just recently hired a cute blonde that was a Christian, and he should stop by the shop some time to check her out! After a men's breakfast at church one Saturday, this man paid me a surprise visit.

It was during the Christmas holidays when he popped in. I was exhausted from working late the night before. I was knee deep in pine branches and my hands were cut and covered with sticky sap. I was wearing old, bummy jeans and went to work that day without any make-up on. I was definitely not my model-best!

When I heard a man's voice asking the receptionist if he could speak with me, I realized he was the person Rick had told me about. I was so embarrassed about the way I looked that I hid under my design counter. I quickly put some lipstick on trying to make myself look more attractive or at least presentable. The lipstick case stuck to my fingers! Then I slowly raised my head up to catch a glimpse of him; he was very attractive. I scurried my way to the back of the shop to scrub my hands and then finally made it to the front counter. After introducing myself, I apologized for my appearance. I probably didn't make a good first impression. I was so mad at Rick for not warning me that this man was on his way over to meet me.

His name was Paul. He was tall and handsome with dark hair and a warm smile. He spoke calmly with a gentle voice and was very humble and polite. He seemed to be sophisticated as he was wearing his stylish Ralph Lauren attire. I was impressed with his personality and his preppy appearance. Paul was quite a contrast to Lance's trendy look and long blond hair. Paul was a businessman, while Lance was a Christian rocker, but they both possessed unique qualities that attracted me to them. Lance and I had remained friends over time, but after meeting Paul, I knew I needed to close that door completely.

At the time I met Paul, he was actually dating another woman that he enjoyed being with, but knew they would not have a future together for spiritual reasons.

My initial conversation with Paul was very engaging. We spoke about the churches we attended and the ministries we were involved in. The flower shop was very busy for the holidays, so the other designers gave me "the look" to get back to work. I liked Paul already and hated to say goodbye. We ended our conversation by planning a lunch date for some time in January. He said he would call me after he returned from visiting his family; he would be out of town for the holidays. That seemed to be a very long time to wait. I longed to see him again.

**Life is full of changes. For everything that's
ending, something new has just begun.**

CHAPTER 11

Lady in Waiting

Time Reveals God's Sacred Plan.

Wait for the Lord; be strong and take
heart and wait for the Lord.
Psalm 27:14

After the holidays, I anticipated Paul's phone call. I was anxious to speak with him again. I wanted to see if the Lord's divine hand was bringing us together. The holidays were over and I still hadn't heard from him. I felt disappointed and was concerned that he might not be interested in me. But I still had a glimmer of hope in my heart.

Life continued to be a struggle, but staying busy helped take my focus off of wondering about Paul. I was now working two jobs. I was a floral designer by day and gymnastics coach by night. My past experience as a gymnast and coach was now helping me make ends meet. I also organized gym birthday parties on the weekends. It was exhausting but God gave me the strength to persevere. *"I can do everything through him who gives me strength" (Philippians 4:13).* Work was consuming all of my time, leaving little time left for Celia, but worse than that, she felt like a yo-yo being tossed back and forth between two parents.

When visitation time came, we would meet half way at the turnpike station to exchange our besieged little girl. On the way to be with her father, she would often hold her stomach, complaining that she felt sick. I would remind her of the Scripture, *"Cast your anxiety on him because he cares for you" (1 Peter 5:7)*. She would get out of one car, get in the other, and drive away. Andre and I rarely exchanged words; when we did, they were not pleasant. His tirades and wicked behavior continued, and I was still afraid of him.

I cried for Celia and prayed fervently for her protection. I hated letting her go with him - I knew her heart and loyalty were torn between us. She lived two different lives with two different identities. She often came back to me feeling angry and was disrespectful. I know this is one reason why God hates divorce. The children become the innocent victims and suffer gravely.

Celia had already suffered so many grueling episodes in her life. When her father and I talked negatively about each other, it crushed her spirit even more. I always asked her about the visitation time she had with her father. I was concerned about her safety and general well being. She usually reacted with hostility to my interrogation and tried to convince me that everything was fine. I knew that it was not. I didn't trust Andre.

This was such a difficult time of my life. I was working two jobs, emotionally falling apart and trying to take care of Celia. I held on to the promise of the Scripture that God would restore the years that the locusts had eaten. Three different people had spoken this verse from the book of Joel to me. I believed that this was a confirmation that would eventually come to pass. It saddened me that much of my life and Celia's had been lost and stripped away.

God knew my heart's desire to be in a loving, Christ-centered relationship. I wanted God's design for marriage to be modeled for Celia. I reinforced the fact that what she had seen between her father and I was not God's intention for a marriage relationship. I also explained that living together before marriage was not in God's will and had many negative consequences.

After meeting Paul and hearing my boss Rick speak so highly of him, I really wanted to see him again. Several weeks went by before I even heard from Paul. I wondered if his first impression of me drove him away, or perhaps he was interested in another woman. I was losing hope, but not completely, when the phone rang one Saturday evening and I heard the sound of his voice. He finally called me, explaining that his work required a lot of travel in the states and abroad. I was comforted by his comment, and felt reassured that he was still interested! He asked me if I would like to meet him the following week, at a local restaurant for a casual lunch. Without hesitation, I willingly said yes!

When that special day came, I had some major wardrobe dilemmas! The way I looked when he first met me was a disaster. I knew he was very conservative so I didn't want to look too artsy. I made a special trip to Jenna's closet to investigate her wardrobe. I ended up wearing black pants, a white button down blouse with a cute little vest. My friends at the flower shop warned me to never order pasta on a first date. I took their advice seriously, pasta was messy and I didn't want to spill it on Jenna's white shirt anyway.

When I arrived at the restaurant, I was really nervous. Paul was standing by the hostess, and when he saw me, he gave me a sweet smile. We talked for at least an hour before we even ordered our meal, and of course, I did not order pasta! Our conversation was relaxed and engaging. I thought that was a good sign. I felt that God was doing something in my heart, and I was hoping he felt it too. Our connection began with our love for Jesus. It grew with shared seasons of sorrow over sudden losses in both of our lives: the loss of my little Leena and the loss of his parents and a grandmother from a tragic car accident. This occurred when he was only eleven years old. We also had both experienced the agony of divorce. Paul had wanted children with his ex-wife, but she was more interested in having a career than a family.

As we slowly dated over a period of time, we seemed compatible, but we instinctively had our guard up, not wanting to get hurt again. When my wall started to come down, his stayed up, causing our relationship to move much slower than I had hoped. It was months before he and Celia even met, partially because of his extensive traveling for work. He was kind with her but reserved, knowing it wasn't easy for her to share her mom.

He also knew how attached Celia had become to my previous boyfriend, Lance. He was afraid to get too close too quickly with either one of us, in case things did not move forward. He was very cautious, and wanted to take things slowly.

After a few months of occasional dating, Paul revealed to me that he was still seeing a woman he had met before me. I was crushed! I assertively told him that if he wanted to continue dating me, he would have to let her go. At times, I questioned if Paul was really attracted to me. He was a conservative, intelligent businessman and I was the free-spirited artsy type, but I held on to the hope that opposites attract and this relationship would be fulfilling. There was definitely an attraction between us, but I was concerned that he was still holding on to someone else. Sometimes it's just hard to let go, but he finally did.

After we had dated for several months, Paul asked me to take a Christian compatibility test. He eagerly wanted to know if there was a chance for us to share a future together.

Even though our relationship was being built on a solid faith in Christ, it didn't necessarily mean that we would have the perfect marriage. I was nervous about taking the test because I liked him so much. I even considered gearing my answers to be more like him so that our results would show a greater compatibility. Despite my apprehension, I agreed to do it. I didn't even cheat! Our results actually said we were a good match, and there was a chance for a promising future. One thing we shared was a strong desire to have more children. I knew Paul would be a great father and I longed for another child, especially after losing my daughter.

One evening, I invited Paul to my apartment for dinner. After we finished the meal, Celia exclaimed, "My mom must really like you because she doesn't cook for anyone, not even me!" We all laughed because it was the truth. My work schedule was crazy and we usually either ate on the go or at my sister Jenna's house. The fast food was not the healthiest, but Jenna's meals were delicious and nutritious.

Paul and I started spending more and more time together. I relished every moment I spent with Paul and wondered if I was even deserving of him. I had been beaten down so badly, I lost much of my confidence and self-worth even though Paul was always well mannered and treated me like a lady. We did a lot of fun things together and went out on many romantic dinner dates. We would lay out in the sun by his pool then relax in the jacuzzi by the light of the moon. We enjoyed going to Christian concerts and strolling through weekend jazz and art festivals holding hands.

This friendship grew into a romance, but he was still guarding his heart. We waltzed to that familiar dating dance. The more I showed my feelings of love, the more he backed away, and the more I backed away, the more he would pursue me.

After almost a year of dating, I completely opened up to him and let my guard down. I told him that I cared very deeply for him and then said the "L" word. I wanted to hear how he felt about me but he just couldn't say it. I was becoming very impatient. With tears in his eyes, he told me that he wanted to love me. Then he tried to express his feelings about why he was so hesitant. He had some concerns about our future, was still wounded from the past, and just wasn't ready to make a commitment. He told me he prayed faithfully for God's direction in our lives and even sought Christian counseling.

Paul's indecisiveness caused me to question if he really cared about me, so I told him we needed some space for a while. He was very hurt and felt rejected but never fought for our relationship. This hurt me even more.

Another Christian man who had crossed my path was showing an unwavering interest in me. His name was Tom. I was curious and wondered if this was God's divine intervention. He had suddenly come into my life and was pursuing me with hopeful determination. He kept enticing me to forget about Paul and to give him a chance. Even though I was curious about Tom, I never stopped caring about Paul.

This song reflects what I was feeling about Paul and our relationship at that time.

This Moment in Time

(Verse One)
Open your eyes, don't hide in the shadows in the dark,
Open your eyes, then open your heart.
The day will break, then tomorrow you'll fly away,
Do you hear love's whispers when we are apart?

(Chorus)
And as time goes by, I don't know where we're going,
There's no promise in your eyes,
Are we just living for the moment, just for the moment,
This moment in time.

(Verse Two)
The hopeless romantic and dreamer that I am,
Always thinking that I need a man,
I lie in your arms, and then
you're dancing on a distant shore,
Why are you searching for something more?

(Chorus)
And as time goes by, I don't know where we're going,
There's no promise in your eyes,
Are we just living for the moment, just for the moment.
This moment in time.
Are you only mine, for this moment in time?

I obviously wanted to be with Paul for more than a few moments in time. Another Christmas was upon us, which marked our one-year anniversary from the time we first met.

This other man I started dating pursued me wholeheartedly. He even bought me an expensive guitar for Christmas. I couldn't believe it! He told me to use it for the Lord even if things didn't work out between us. He seemed to be infatuated with me and was a little obsessive. Ironically, he sent me extravagant flowers while I was working at a flower shop. He frequently left love notes on my car. I was flattered but concerned that he was a bit eccentric. His behavior was very demonstrative. He even started talking about marriage. Now I had a guy that was moving too fast. I started to realize that his tactics had ulterior motives. In comparison, Paul was very reserved, remarkably displaying an abundance of self-control.

There was a big red flag when Tom became angry and hostile toward me for not devoting enough time to him. I quickly ended the relationship, discerning that he definitely was not for me. It was an all-too familiar scenario. I had already been on that rollercoaster ride and it was time to jump off and run the other way! I wasn't about to go down that path again.

The time away from Paul made me miss him and want him even more. After I ended it with Tom, I called Paul from a pay phone at a restaurant and asked him to meet me there. I was hoping he would, and was happy when he came right away. After I told him what happened with Tom, he was relieved. He affectionately held my hand for most of the evening. We were back together as if we had never separated.

It was my perception that Paul really wanted the type of woman who was driven and successful in the business world. I even tried changing my style of dress and wore tailored clothes for a while. I toned down my exuberant expression of fashion, thinking he might be more attracted to me. On one occasion, he picked me up for a date wearing blue jeans and a cool shirt, not his usual attire. I was wearing a tailored, business-like outfit, thinking it would appease him. It was too funny!

His wall finally came down when I gave up the façade and allowed myself to be completely authentic, the way God created me to be. Paul started to see me in a different light, dropping his preconceived image of the perfect match. He was falling in love with me and started to really show it. He told me that my love for children moved him, and he could see the fruit of the spirit in me. *"But the fruit of the Spirit is love, joy, peace, patience, kindness, goodness, faithfulness, gentleness and self control" (Galatians 5:22).* He finally had peace that the Lord brought us together.

We both read several books on relationships from well-known Christian authors. They advised having a two-year courtship before getting married. We were following their advice and believed we had the three main ingredients needed to have a great marriage: a commitment to the Lord, a foundation built on friendship, and a strong chemistry. Paul hadn't proposed to me yet, but said, "I love you" more than once and was taking our relationship more seriously. A co-worker at the flower shop once told me that when he finally says, "I love you," he is really going to mean it.

I had been waiting to renew my apartment lease in hope of Paul and I moving forward towards marriage. Friends at church told me not to give up on him, to be patient and wait for God's perfect timing. I started to focus more on God than on Paul by reading the Bible and praying more frequently. I finally let go and put it all in God's hands. I knew God would take care of Celia and me no matter what happened. Paul was a man of integrity, an elder in the church, and well respected for his Christ-like character. I knew he was one in a million, so I continued to wait. I wondered if Paul would ever ask me to marry him. I was still a lady in waiting.

One evening, Paul surprised me by taking me out to the most fabulous, romantic restaurant on the beach. After a wonderful dinner, we walked along the shore. The moonlight sparkled like diamonds, dancing upon the waves. He then carefully pulled a velvety red rose out of his jacket and said that he wanted to ask me something. I had no idea that he was about to propose. I thought he was going to ask me if I wanted to go to a movie or what I wanted to do for the rest of the evening.

With his gentle spirit, he spoke slowly and softly asking me to marry him and be his wife forever. He promised to always love and cherish me. I anxiously replied saying, "You don't know how long I've waited for you to ask me. Yes, I'll marry you and I will love you forever!" With tears in our eyes, we embraced and kissed under the light of the moon. We both felt the peace and presence of the Lord. It was God's appointed time.

Paul gave me the rose in lieu of a ring, explaining that because I was so creative he thought I might like to design the ring myself. I was touched that he truly loved me for who I was. It was all in God's perfect timing. When I took my main focus off of Paul and onto the Lord, He gave me the desire of my heart.

Paul started to reach out to Celia, but it took time for her to warm up to him. He took her out to dinner to ask her "permission" to marry her mom. He assured her that he wanted to be part of the family, not take me from her. He promised to take care of her, but she still felt a distance between them and was skeptical of this man she barely knew. Up to this point, he only held a small place in her heart even though he was about to become her stepfather. I knew she would eventually warm up to him. Paul was a wonderful man with many fine qualities. He was firm in principle yet tender regarding his heart's intent. He loved both of us dearly.

Paul and I eagerly anticipated our wedding day. We had a lot to prepare for, the flowers, food, music, and all the accompaniments. I wrote a special love song to Paul and planned to perform it on my guitar at the reception. Jenna and Mark graciously offered their beautiful home to us for the ceremony and reception. It was a joy for them to host our celebration.

Coming from large families, we wanted to keep the guest list as minimal as possible. We both wanted a simple but lovely celebration. We planned to have the ceremony outside on the patio just before sunset. We chose the music carefully from Christian CDs and picked songs for a live band to perform. We hired a professional photographer and someone to capture the moments on video.

As the search for the perfect wedding gown began, Jenna and Celia joined in on the fun of this endeavor. I was looking for a dress that would accentuate my artistic vintage style and personality. Our first stop was a boutique called Sacred Threads. I immediately fell in love with an ivory wedding gown that was exquisitely made of raw silk. The top of the dress was a corset, accented with cream lace, and embellished with pearls. There was a bustle in the back made of silk fabric roses and a small flowing train. We found a beautiful lavender dress for Celia that was also made of a raw silk fabric. She looked so happy, prancing around the dressing room and admiring herself in the mirror. There was no need to look any further. It was a glorious time making the plans and preparations, and it was all coming together.

I wasn't young and naïve, hoping for a fortunate future. I wasn't blinded and infatuated with a man I barely knew. I was genuinely in love with a man who was also my friend. This incredible man looked out for my best interest and never wanted to hurt me. He loved God with all his heart, soul and mind. He walked the talk. Jesus' love was reflected in his eyes and in his character. I knew without a shadow of a doubt, this time was forever!

***Don't give up hope or lose heart, God's
timing is always perfect.***

CHAPTER 12

Cream Lace with Roses

He Gives Blessings Beyond Measure and His Love Is a Priceless Treasure.

*Trust in the Lord, and do good; dwell in the land
and enjoy safe pasture. Delight yourself in the Lord,
and He will give you the desires of your heart.
Psalm 37:3-4*

Our hearts rejoiced as the day approached when our lives would become one. On that sacred day, we stood beneath a floral archway covered with ivy, silk ribbon and cream roses. The sunset was picturesque, with a spectacular display of colors. Everything was simply beautiful. There was an extravagant floral arrangement in the center of the pool with floating candles surrounding it. I designed topiaries for the table centerpieces in whitewash clay pots, and the food we had catered was artistically displayed and delicious.

Paul was dazzling in his black tuxedo, and I felt very elegant in my gorgeous wedding gown. I designed my bridal bouquet with cream roses and fragrant fillers. The stems were wrapped with ribbon that was trimmed in pearls. Celia's bouquet was made with lavender roses and ribbon that matched her dress perfectly. One of the sweetest parts of our wedding ceremony was when Paul put a ring on Celia's finger and promised to love her forever also.

As our vows were exchanged, they were intertwined with our favorite Scriptures. Paul didn't just say, "I do," he said, "I do forever!" We cherished each other and were excited to begin our lives as one. *"And the two will become one flesh" (Ephesians 5:31).* The ceremony and evening were more than sublime. We were lost in each other's eyes. He was the man I had longed for and the love of my life. Paul couldn't stop telling me how much he loved and adored me. I felt like I was dancing on a cloud.

This is a song that I wrote for him and sang with my guitar at the reception.

Dancing On A Cloud

(Verse One)
If I am dreaming, don't wake me up,
For I am dancing on a cloud up in the sky,
And every morning when I wake to see your face,
I'll be lifted up on heaven's wings and fly.

(Chorus)
And my heart will always love you,
And my arms will never let go,
You are a gift that God has given to me,
My love for you overflows.

(Verse Two)
In cream lace with roses, in these sacred moments,
You take my hand and make my life your own,
As we're joined together, we know forever,
From this day on, we will never be alone.

(Verse Three)
As we turn the pages, the story changes,
But our love will last and stand the test of time,
We look to the Savior 'cause this life's a vapor,
We share the glory of His everlasting love divine.

(Chorus) If I am dreaming, don't wake me up.

That extraordinary night ended with a slow dance in anticipation of spending that first night together to consummate our love. It took a lot of effort on both our parts to resist the temptation to have sex before we were married. Staying faithful to our conviction, we waited until our wedding night to enjoy the sacred gift of intimacy.

On our first night together, we knelt down beside the bed and thanked God for the awesome love we had for each other. We asked Him to bless our union and to give us the gift of a child. He was faithful in answering both of these prayers.

We spent our honeymoon in Carmel Valley, California and had a fabulous time. It was first class all the way. We stayed at an elaborate chateau on an equestrian estate. The gardens were gorgeous, exploding with colors - like an artist's pallet. It was incredible!

We drove along the Pacific Coast Highway and were amazed at the breathtaking, magnificent view. We dined on mountaintops, toured vineyards, visited art museums, and warmed our hearts and bodies by flaming fireplaces. It was an exquisite honeymoon, more marvelous than I could have ever imagined! We were so in love and enjoyed each other's company tremendously. It was a dream come true! He was the most wonderful man I have ever known, kind, gentle and considerate. He treated me with so much love and dignity. I had total peace and *knew* that Paul was a gift from God. Through God's love, grace and mercy, He bestowed upon me heavenly blessings. *"Every good and perfect gift is from above, coming down from the Father of the heavenly lights, who does not change like shifting shadows"* *(James 1:17)*.

After our incredible honeymoon, Celia and I moved into Paul's house. Our home was beautiful and I enjoyed giving it a woman's touch. I expected the transition to be difficult for Celia but things were going rather smoothly. Andre was working out of town, which gave Celia and Paul a chance to develop their new relationship. Unfortunately though, Paul was still traveling periodically with his job so just as they would get closer, he would have to leave again. She resented this new way of life because her family was still fractured and now she had to divide her loyalty between two fathers.

A few weeks after we were married, I went with Paul on a business trip to London. It was like a second honeymoon for us. While he worked during the day, I explored the city and shopped, taking in all of the beautiful sights and history. We met in the evenings for dinner and entertainment – it was so much fun!

After our London trip, we flew to visit his brother and family who were living in another European city as missionaries. We stayed at a quaint hotel near their home. This was where one of our prayers was answered. God gave us the desires of our hearts. I conceived and would give birth at the age of 40, which was a miracle to me.

I had a healthy pregnancy, but it was different from my other pregnancies. I grew tired more easily and experienced severe backaches. When the time came for a sonogram, I already knew in my heart that it was a boy. After Leena died, I always felt that if I ever had another child, God would give me a boy. Celia had hoped for a baby sister and I understood why.

On the day I was having the sonogram, Celia went to the school office and called me at the hospital. When I told her it was a boy, she started to cry and hung up on me. The school nurse asked her why she was upset and tried to calm her down. The nurse was concerned that something was wrong with the baby, but Celia exclaimed that it was a boy!

When the time came for the baby to be delivered, I was more than ready. I was determined not to feel the pain in childbirth that I had experienced before. I had an epidural before they even induced me or any contractions began. It was a beautiful and relatively pain-free birthing experience.

When the baby was born, the nurse laid him on my chest and I cried tears of joy. Paul cut the cord and we reveled in this gift from God. We named him Luke, which means "bringer of light." He was a new light in our lives and we welcomed him with much love and admiration.

Luke was a beautiful, happy baby and the spitting image of Paul. Having another child was very healing. It filled a vacancy in my heart, even though no one could ever replace Leena. The tragedy I had experienced caused me to be very protective of Luke, even to the point of never feeding him an apple. I was hesitant to ever eat one again myself. On the anniversaries of Leena's birth and death, there was an aching deep in my heart, but I never wanted to return to the depths of pain I had wallowed in before. Occasionally, God gave me the gift of seeing her in my dreams. I was grateful for those precious moments to be with her again; they seemed so real.

As Luke grew into a toddler, his adorable and witty personality kept us constantly entertained. Sadly, it took some time for Celia to warm up to him. Perhaps it was because someone else was taking me away from her, or she was afraid to get too close in fear of losing him, as she had lost her little sister.

Celia was now thirteen years old, very mature, intelligent, tall and beautiful. Occasionally when we were out together, some people thought Celia was Luke's mother. After those comments, she didn't want to hold him in public anymore. Her withdrawal from him became even worse when Andre told her that Luke was not really her brother. This wicked remark confused Celia. Whenever Andre's actions or words did not align with his professed faith, it caused her to question her own spirituality. We tried to help her by taking her to a Christian counselor. We hoped she would express her feelings from all she had been through and still had to deal with.

Despite Andre's negative remarks, Celia loved babies and soon began mothering and smothering Luke with love and affection. Sometimes I had to remind Celia that I was Luke's mother! As he grew and started to talk, she insisted Luke call her "sis" just as Leena did.

By this time Jenna had her third child, another boy whom she named Josiah. Luke loved him and they were buds! The whole boy thing was new to me, but I adjusted to the noise of racecars, wrestling matches, and large collections of rocks and sticks. There was never a dull moment with Jenna and her boys. I thanked God for them.

Luke was also blessed that God provided a special man to be his adopted grandfather. This incredible man had worked with Paul in the past, and they eventually became best friends. He never had any children, so he treated Paul as if he were his own son. He was a great father figure. Paul really loved and respected him. His wife passed away from a brain tumor shortly before Luke was born. Luke's life brought him so much joy that it actually helped his grieving and healing process. He poured his love into Luke from the time he was born and has ever since. They share a closeness that touches my heart.

Paul was such an incredible husband. He was also an awesome father. He was always calm and patient with Luke. He was definitely a hands-on dad. From changing diapers to rocking him to sleep, he had the dad thing down and loved every minute of it. Luke had him wrapped around his little pinky! Paul read a lot of books and Bible stories to him, raising him in the admonition of the Lord.

As the years passed, they enjoyed playing various sports and board games. They did many activities together. Luke definitely inherited Paul's intelligence. They looked so much alike and had so many similarities; it was evident that they belonged to each other.

As time passed, not only did Celia and Luke develop a strong bond, but Paul and Celia also grew to love each other immensely. We were truly blessed as a family. Paul and I had a great marriage. We read the Bible and prayed together nearly every day, shared common interests, and took fabulous trips together. We rarely fought and if we ever disagreed, we discussed the issue and worked things out in a peaceful manner. We even had "nice" fights occasionally over who would do the dishes. Sometimes I gave in and let him win! It was easy to submit to Paul's leadership; he loved me as Christ loved the church.

"I will repay you for the years the locusts have eaten" (Joel 2:25). God had restored the years that the locusts had eaten but nothing in this life is perfect. The teenage years with Celia were very challenging. She was fighting for her independence, Andre was still trying to control her, and she was experiencing peer pressure. With all these trials and tribulations, we became prayer warriors. The Lord had us on our knees, even on our faces before Him at times, asking for wisdom and guidance. God was faithful in getting us through the tumultuous times. We knew that with God in our lives, we could overcome anything.

Celia's relationship with Andre was still rocky, but as a young adult, she was learning to stand her ground with him. He was still her father and she loved him unconditionally. He passed on his culinary skills to her, and she developed a passion for the art of cooking. She always tried to see the good in him despite all the terrible things he had done in the past.

I prayed many times, asking God to help me to forgive Andre. We tried to make peace a few times throughout the years but anger and damaged emotions kept bringing us back to a place of strife. We must choose to forgive, but even when we do, the healing process can take a long time. When we don't forgive, it is like a poison that afflicts our own souls. *"And when you stand praying, if you hold anything against anyone, forgive him, so that you father in heaven may forgive you your sins"* (Mark 11:25).

Andre remarried soon after I married Paul. He repeated the impetuous pattern with his new wife and her two young boys. Celia was deeply disturbed by this. It triggered bad memories and opened up wounds that had left emotional scars. It saddened me that even after a long intense course on domestic violence, Andre didn't change. This was obviously a stronghold of abuse that he was not able to admit or overcome.

This repeated behavior made Celia come to the realization of many truths. For years she had blocked out these wearisome times and was in denial of the horrific experiences from her childhood. She drew closer to me as a result of this revelation. I felt closer to her too. Celia sought help again from different counselors during these trying times. I'm sure it was therapeutic for her just to release her feelings.

Andre had tried to manipulate her into believing that I was the bad one for leaving him. No one should ever tolerate any form of abuse. I knew that I had made many mistakes – the first was falling for him, a man I hardly knew. I had little self worth and tried to find it in a man. I agonized over hurting Don and harbored resentment towards Andre for controlling me. I needed a Savior. After I came to the cross, my sins were forgiven. Jesus paid the price for me. I now had the promise of heaven and my name was written in the Lamb's Book of Life. I praise God for that!

I believe all the mistakes I made and lessons learned were part of my journey that God redeemed. He allowed trials and suffering in my life to draw me closer to Him. He gave me beauty for ashes. As painful as it was, it was all worth it. Coming into a relationship with God through Jesus Christ, having my two daughters and a new life with Paul and Luke has brought me many blessings beyond measure.

I continued to praise God, singing my heart out in the music ministry. I was the worship leader at our church for several years and tried to involve Celia as much as possible by singing with the praise team and performing worship dances. She inherited these gifts from me, but she was sometimes reluctant to use them. This is a song that I wrote and sang to her at church after her high school graduation.

Daughter of the King

(Verse One)
When your heart aches my heart is breaking,
When there's no smiles left for faking,
I can see right through,
There is still a beautiful you,
He made you in a most amazing way,
He gave to me a gift I know I never can repay.

(Chorus)
Daughter of the King
Praise His name in every song you sing
Daughter of the King
Only mine for such a short time
You're the daughter of the King

(Verse Two)
When you smile my heart rejoices,
If you don't always make the right choices,
I will always love you anyway,
Get down on my knees and pray,
There is power in a mother's prayer,
His angels will protect you,
From the crazy world out there.

(Verse Three)
When you fly away I will be crying,
If your dreams are ever dying,
Just remember to whom you belong,
God our Father's arms are strong,
He will always be your guiding light,
And in your eyes I can see,
His loving is shining bright.

Now, in the autumn of my life, I wonder how all those years could have passed me by so quickly. It seems like I lived many different lives. As I wake each morning and stand before the Lord, I am grateful for the hardships that have strengthened me and have drawn me closer to Him. *"Hear, O Lord, and be merciful to me; O Lord, be my help. You turned my wailing into dancing; you removed my sackcloth and clothed me with joy, that my heart may sing to you and not be silent. O Lord my God, I will give you thanks forever"* (Psalm 30:10-12).

> **Praise the Lord through trials and triumphs, finish the race and keep the faith. Never stray from the narrow path ... it leads to paradise.**

CHAPTER 13

The Autumn of My Life

Treasure Each Moment As If It Was Your Last - This Life Is Like a Vapor, and Paradise Is Not That Far Away.

*Weeping may remain for a night, but
rejoicing comes in the morning.
Psalm 30:5*

In the shadows of the night, I lay awake in bed tossing and turning relentlessly. I just couldn't sleep. Besides the hot flashes and cold sweats, many thoughts were invading my mind. My husband's job, my daughter away at college, and all the things I needed to accomplish that week. My back ached and my joints were stiff. I was slightly bothered by the fact that during the day I was using more concealer to fill in the lines on my face. I needed to get a grip and just face it – I was in the autumn of my life.

I finally fell back asleep just in time for the alarm to go off. I rose from the tangled sheets to conquer the tasks of my daily routine. That all too familiar song that echoes a woman's existence. Meals, laundry, errands, groceries, and the lists go on. Before the busyness of my morning began, I stepped outside to pick up the newspaper for my husband who worked so hard to provide for our family. I hoped and prayed that our neighbors wouldn't catch a glimpse of me in my frumpy pajamas. I had major bed head, wasn't wearing a bra (gravity had not been kind), and had not yet put my face on for the day. I was a frightful disheveled sight!

As my bare feet touched the ground, a cool breeze blew through me, whispering that autumn had arrived. I paused for a moment, to embrace the season's splendor, while craving a spiced pumpkin latte. Suddenly, something even more satisfying captured the essence of my entire being, filling my senses beyond measure. It was the Rauch, which in Hebrew means, wind and also Holy Spirit. John 3:8 says, *"The wind blows wherever it pleases. You hear its sound, but you cannot tell where it comes from or where it is going. So it is with everyone born of the Spirit."*

While feeling the presence of the Lord, He allowed me to see through spiritual eyes. Flashbacks from my life flooded my mind. The reflection of His love gave me peace as His living water filled my soul. *"See I am doing a new thing! Now it springs up; do you not perceive it, I am making a way in the desert and streams in the wasteland" (Isaiah 43:19).*

He showed me that as I stood there in the autumn of my life, change was inevitable. Sometimes the waters were smooth sailing and sometimes there were rough seas. Regardless, I had peace and joy knowing that Jesus rescued my sinking soul. As it says in John 16:33, *"I have told you these things so that in me you may have peace. In this world you will have trouble but take heart I have overcome the world."* When we abide in Him, we can overcome any trials and changes that continue to come our way.

The Lord continued to speak to me. This time He gave me a vision of the deepest sufferings in my life and how He had carried me through them. These sufferings included: the agony of a volatile marriage that ended in divorce, the death of both my parents whom I deeply loved, and my life's worst tragedy – the death of my precious little daughter.

I could clearly see the day of her burial. I approached the cemetery with my seven-year-old daughter and my sister Jenna who was pregnant with her second child. I saw myself gazing out the car window, still in shock. My family and close friends were weeping as they hovered around the small white coffin. My little girl Leena lay silently inside, wearing a green floral print dress that her big sister once wore. Her lifeless arms were wrapped around her favorite baby doll. I hesitated getting out of the car. I didn't want to face the burial ceremony. As my feet touched the ground, my knees buckled from beneath me, and I started to collapse. My sisters ran to help me. They led me to the coffin and open grave where Leena's body would be buried.

The coldness of death stung like a winter storm. I started to shiver. Leena's father and I didn't even exist to each other, even though this little child had belonged to both of us. Near the end of the ceremony, in the stillness of the air, a cool breeze started to blow and encircled us all. My friend Nina leaned gently toward me and whispered: "Do you feel it? It's the breath of God, the Holy Spirit is here." It was the Ruach, the Comforter. I felt God's presence and desperately embraced His peace. At that moment, I started to worship God by softly singing Amazing Grace.

That vision slowly faded from my memory and my mind returned back to the cool ground where I stood in my front yard. I thanked God for the peace of His Spirit, and for all the blessings in my life. My heart rejoiced in knowing that I will see Leena again. This life is like a vapor and paradise is not that far away. *"Why, you do not even know what will happen tomorrow. What is your life? For you are a mist that appears for a little while and then vanishes away"* (James 4:14).

Our lives are woven together by threads of many colors. Only our Creator sees the beauty in the making of the final artwork of His masterpiece. Like a tapestry, on one side, the threads appear to be knotted and tangled. On the other side, the tapestry reveals the beauty of His glorious purpose and completion of His hand upon our lives.

"And we know that in all things God works for the good of those who love him, who have been called according to his purpose" (Romans 8:28).

Soaring

(Verse One)
As the wind blows through the tallest trees,
The flowers dance with the autumn leaves,
Changing moods,
Changes all around,
The air is cool, the fragrance sweet,
I feel a chill beneath my feet,
I can hear the world,
In every little sound.

(Chorus)
We are soaring with every season
With every day,
We are singing every song,
Along the way.

(Verse Two)
As the moments fly we reminisce,
Did our dreams foresee a love as good as this,
Will tomorrow bring
The things we're hoping for?
Time is like an hourglass,
We're passing through and moving fast,
Always reaching out
And wanting something more.
(Verse Three)
As we share our lives, we grow as one,
Like the shining moon like the golden sun,
Like the stars above,
We are meant to be here,

Forever we will always keep,
Each other close with feelings deep,
As we travel through,
Life's laughter and its tears.

God's love will warm you in the winter storms;
You will blossom with His beauty in the spring;
The Son will illuminate your summer days; and,
His arms will embrace you through autumn's changes.

EPILOGUE

God's Appointed Time

In the process of preparing to write this book, I came across a love letter Andre had written to me, as shared in my story at the end of Chapter One.

October 7, 1986 5:45PM

My Dearest and Beautiful Love Ashlyn,

I love you so much. My love is so intense that sometimes, just looking in your eyes can make me cry. I feel that your love is so precious, so sensitive, and so pure it could make me melt. I am so proud of our love. I want us to love each other more and more everyday of our lives until the day we die with that same pure intensity. I am going to marry you, have children with you and be with you forever! Andre

Ten years later on **October 7, 1996, at 5:45PM,** our beautiful baby girl Leena left this earth for eternity to be in the arms of her heavenly Father. When I found the letter and read it, I was stunned! I realized the date and time of the letter were exactly the same date and time of our daughter's death! As an overwhelming heaviness came over me, my body became weak and the letter fell from my trembling hands. My soul was stricken with pain. My heart was pierced. Rivers of tears invaded my eyes and I shook uncontrollably. Baffled by the connection of these dates, I knew this could not be a mysterious coincidence. It was so unfathomable! I didn't understand the connection but it eventually brought me to a place of peace.

As it says in Ecclesiastes 3:1-8:

"There is a time for everything,
and a season for every activity under heaven:
a time to be born and a time to die,
a time to plant and a time to uproot,
a time to kill and a time to heal,
a time to tear down and a time to build,
a time to weep and a time to laugh,
a time to mourn and a time to dance,
a time to scatter stones
and a time to gather them,
a time to embrace and a time to refrain,
a time to search and a time to give up,
a time to keep and a time to throw away,
a time to tear and a time to mend,
a time to be silent and a time to speak,
a time to love and a time to hate,
a time for war and a time for peace."

As you venture through life's journey here on earth, remember that every season of your life has a purpose. We all suffer through trials and difficulties in this life. Everyone has a story. This book is my life's journey, but my story will continue until I enter into paradise. I pray that those who have been through similar circumstances will see the light of hope that the Lord has given me to press on. Whatever *your* story is, however painful or glorious, God has a purpose and plan for your life. No matter what mistakes you have made or sins you may have committed, God is always there to forgive you. In Jesus, there is always hope. Even in our darkest times, He is our light and our salvation!

FINAL WORDS

Years ago, at the moment I surrendered my heart to Jesus, I felt a super-natural peace - a peace that surpasses understanding. I knew I needed a Savior and I could never be good enough to earn my way into heaven. Jesus paid the price for me just as it says in John 3:16: *"For God so loved the world that he gave his one and only Son, that whoever believes in him shall not perish but have eternal life."* I asked Him to come into my heart and be the Lord of my life. I was born again - once of the flesh and then of the Spirit. Now His Spirit dwells within me as my comforter and my guide. This life still has many troubles, but I rejoice in knowing the Lord will always be with me and that this earth is not my final home.

If you feel God tugging at your heart, you can pray a simple salvation prayer like the following:

> *Heavenly Father, forgive me for my sins. I need a Savior.*
> *Thank you for sending your Son Jesus to pay the price for my*
> *sins through His death on the cross. I surrender my life to you.*
> *As I become a new creature in Christ, guide me by the power*
> *of Your Holy Spirit. I pray this in the name of Jesus. Amen.*

Your prayer must be a heart felt decision to follow after Jesus Christ. It is the most important decision you will ever make! It determines your eternity. I am so glad I surrendered my life to the Lord. Nothing compares to the peace He has given me, and the hope of heaven where I will be reunited with my loved ones. Leena is waiting for me there in paradise.

It is never too late to accept the Lord. As the thief exclaimed on the cross just before his death:

> "*Then he said, Jesus, remember me when you come into your kingdom. Jesus answered him, assuredly, I tell you the truth, today you will be with me in paradise" (Luke 23:42-43).*

EXPRESSIONS OF PAIN AND PEACE

Sharing Your Grief Can Bring Healing and Peace.

*And to provide for those who grieve in Zion - to bestow on
them a crown of beauty instead of ashes, the oil of gladness
instead of mourning, and a garment of praise instead of a
spirit of despair. They will be called oaks of righteousness,
a planting of the Lord for the display of his splendor.
Isaiah 61:3*

When my heart can let go of
What was once mine to behold
And trust in the hand
Of the Master's plan.
The sweet song of freedom
Will release the chain
That holds my heart captive
In a chamber of pain.
                    -Ashlyn Lark

In the depths of my indescribable pain and endless restless nights, my
thoughts were being consumed by the loss and absence of my little baby
Leena. On my quest for solace, powerful emotions invaded my inmost
being. This chapter contains a collection of poetry from these expressions

of pain, and reveals the peace that supernaturally sustained me through my journey, starting with Celia's expression of sorrow and her hope of heaven.

Celia's Poetry

Rainy Day

On a rainy day
My tears don't go away
Because of my sorrow
Of my sister's death.
For being so young
And so sweet
My heart breaks for her
Because she's not mine to keep.

The Cloud

Somewhere over the rainbow
There's a cloud, a cloud
With my baby sister on it
And she's screaming loud!

One day she'll scream
"I love you, Sissy"
And on that day
I'll know she's OK.

Smiling Down

When I am in my imaginary land
I am floating on clouds so high
When I float so high, I can see the sky
I can see my little sister smiling down
And I know I miss her
Oh so bad, oh so bad

When I am in my imaginary land
It feels the greatest
When I see the gates of heaven
Waiting there for me
And some of my friends and family
Smiling down
And I know that I miss them
Oh so bad, oh so bad

Then I can see Jesus smiling at me
It touches my heart when I see His smiling face
He stares at me and He sees that I love Him
And I run to Him and my sister
She smiles at me and oh I miss her
Oh I miss her, oh so much and oh so bad

Leena's Song (Celia age 10)

(Verse One)
She was just a beautiful girl
living in an unpleasant world
But she had the family just right for her
She sparkled like gold sparkles, she was a little angel
She was the most perfect sister you'd ever have
She was sweet and she was kind
And the last time I saw her she was so young
Looking like a little butterfly
Fluttering in the sky

(Chorus)
She was smiling like gold sparkling in the skies
Like the little pink rays of sunshine

(Verse Two)
Even though I'll never see her smile
Until we get to those little pink rays of sunshine
And I kissed her goodbye
Not that long before she died
She was a bubbly little child
But a little strong willed too
But she was the best sister
That I ever knew

(Verse Three)
Even though I will miss her so much
And I will remember it's my heart that she touched
She was one of the reasons that I kept living
Now that she's gone I feel there's nothing for me

(Verse Four)
All I have is memories
Life would have no point without these
She laughed and played
Like a little angel
And I will always remember
The kisses and hugs that we shared
She was the greatest sister
I loved her as high as the sky

Ashlyn's Poetry

Fading Fast

My arms are empty, there's no baby to hold,
It is the winter of my heart, the brutal wind is blowing cold.

Seasons change, but for me time stands still,
In the midst of an aching memory, I search for God's will.

Many teardrops of pain, burst forth and bitterly fall,
On a grave where beneath, she lies holding her favorite doll.

This feeling won't leave or elude me, my body is fragile and weak,
I fall to the ground and kiss the hard stone, instead of kissing her cheek.

Restless

Hiding beneath the winter's bitter snow,
A restless spirit longs to sing,
Dreaming of vibrant lovely flowers,
That promise to bloom again in spring.

Longing for a breath of new life,
To revive her from paralyzed gloom,
She hides in darkness waiting for the light,
To illuminate her isolated room.

She desperately screams - dig up the shallow grave,
Bring my baby back to me,
Her soul is buried in a river of tears,
Tormented by elusive memories.

She strives to embrace her baby's beating heart,
So far away from her grasp,
She breaks the silence with moans of agony,
Piercing through her heart's shattered glass.

Broken Pieces

My God, My God, I cry out to you,
For the baby in my womb, that grew and grew.

A miracle of life snatched away in a moment's time,
I never imagined that she'd no longer be mine.

I held her hand, her laughter and her tears,
I thought I would hold her for many years.

The agony of her absence floods my soul,
Pour out your peace, make my broken heart whole.

Prison of Pain

In a prison of pain
I turn to Him,
And He lifts me up
In His arms again.

He knows the torment
Of my tragic loss,
He carried my burdens
As He carried the cross.

Grateful

Until I look into my Savior' eyes,
My mind is filled with many whys.

But I am grateful for when she was mine,
As I reflect upon that precious time.

I treasure the moments, holding them tight,
As I desperately reach for His sacred light.

With each new day that passes by,
He catches the falling tears I cry.

Tears in a Bottle

Lord save my tears in Your bottle,
That I so painfully shed,
Breathe life into me again,
My world seems so dead.

When I need Your living waters,
Let the heavens pour them down,
'Till the grey clouds disappear,
And a rainbow can be found.

The Mystery

Where did you go my little one?
In the presence of the Spirit, the Father and the Son.
Your joy is full while my heart weeps,
Under the ground your little body sleeps.

You're dancing on a pink cloud,
While in anguish my soul bleeds.
I want to turn back the hands of time,
And take care of all your needs.

Now you sing with the angels,
Before His sacred throne.
Do you think about your Mommy?
When I see you, will you be grown?

I bear the pain of this mystery,
And there isn't much left of me.
God is the giver and taker of life,
The anguish cuts deeper than a knife.

Longing

I wake up in hopes to see her face,
Kiss her cheek and feel her embrace.
How I long to see her there,
But she's only a memory in my silent prayer.

All of the moments I had her on earth,
No one could ever measure their worth.
The pain is so real in my daily routine,
No baby to hug, no little mouth to clean.

Toys lay still, an empty shopping cart,
The little dresses she wore, I hold close to my heart.
I want to see her running to me with open arms,
Dazzle me with her smile and all her little charms.

But oh how the days seem so long,
Father God, please help me be strong.
I want her back here with me,
It's so hard to wait till eternity.

I wake up in hopes to see her face,
But not in this time and not in this place,
For she's never coming back to this earthly plane,
How my soul longs to be with her again.

Sacred Peace

Death
Human flesh
Where the soul is no more
Like empty seashells
Washed up to shore
Like the sun setting
To the depths of the sea
Like a breeze
Passing peacefully

> *Expressions from the depths of your soul, are a sweet release that can bring healing to the broken hearted.*

Summary of all Bible verses presented in the book:

All Bible Scripture verses referenced in this book are taken from the New International Version.

James 1:14: *But each one is tempted when, by his own evil desires, he is dragged away and enticed.*

John 14:6: *Jesus answered, I am the Way, and the Truth, and the Life. No one comes to the Father except through Me.*

Psalm 139:13-14: *For You created my inmost being; you knit me together in my mother's womb. I praise You because I am fearfully and wonderfully made.*

Ezekiel 36:26: *I will give you a new heart and put a new spirit in you. I will remove from you your heart of stone and give you a heart of flesh.*

Acts 4:12: *Salvation is found in no one else, for there is no other name under heaven given to men by which we must be saved.*

John 3:1-7: *Now there was a man of the Pharisees named Nicodemus, a member of the Jewish ruling council. ² He came to Jesus at night and said, "Rabbi, we know you are a teacher who has come from God. For no one could perform the miraculous signs you are doing if God were not with him."³ In reply Jesus declared, "I tell you the truth, no one can see the kingdom of God unless he is born again."⁴ "How can a man be born when he is old?" Nicodemus asked, "Surely he cannot enter a second time into his mother's womb to be born!"⁵ Jesus answered, "I tell you the truth, no one can enter the kingdom of God unless he is born of water and the Spirit. ⁶ Flesh gives birth to flesh, but the Spirit gives birth to spirit. ⁷ You should not be surprised at my saying, 'You must be born again.'"*

John 16:33: *I have told you these things, so that in me you may have peace. In this world you will have trouble. But take heart! I have overcome the world.*

Philippians 2:9: *Therefore God exalted Him to the highest place and gave Him the name that is above every name.*

Romans 3:23-24: *For all have sinned and fall short of the glory of God, and are justified freely by his grace through the redemption that came by Christ Jesus.*

Philippians 4:8: *Finally, brothers, whatever is true, whatever is noble, whatever is right, whatever is pure, whatever is lovely, whatever is admirable – if anything is excellent or praiseworthy – think about such things.*

Isaiah 53:5: *But he was pierced for our transgressions, he was crushed for our iniquities; the punishment that brought us peace was upon him, and by his wounds we are healed.*

Mark 11:24: *Therefore I tell you, whatever you ask for in prayer, believe that you have received it, and it will be yours.*

2 Corinthians 9:7: *For God loves a cheerful giver.*

Proverbs 3:5-6: *Trust in the Lord with all your heart and lean not on your own understanding; in all your ways acknowledge him, and he will make your path straight.*

Philippians 4:19: *And my God will meet all your needs according to his glorious riches in Christ Jesus.*

Psalm 27:1: *The Lord is my light and my salvation - whom shall I fear? The Lord is the stronghold of my life – of whom shall I be afraid?*

Psalm 46:1: *God is our refuge and strength, an ever-present help in trouble.*

Psalm 23:4: *Even though I walk through the valley of the shadow of death, I will fear no evil, for you are with me; your rod and your staff, they comfort me.*

2 Samuel 12:23: *But now that he is dead, why should I fast? Can I bring him back again? I will go to him, but he will not return to me.*

2 Corinthians 5:1-9: *For we know that if the earthly tent we live in is destroyed, we have a building from God, an eternal house in heaven, not built by human hands. ² Meanwhile we groan, longing to be clothed instead with our heavenly dwelling, ³ because when we are clothed, we will not be found naked. ⁴ For while we are in this tent, we groan and are burdened, because we do not wish to be unclothed but to be clothed instead with our heavenly dwelling, so that what is mortal may be swallowed up by life. ⁵ Now the one who has fashioned us for this very purpose is God, who has given us the Spirit as a deposit, guaranteeing what is to come. ⁶ Therefore we are always confident and know that as long as we are at home in the body we are away from the Lord. ⁷ For we live by faith, not by sight. ⁸ We are confident, I say, and would prefer to be away from the body and at home with the Lord. ⁹ So we make it our goal to please him, whether we are at home in the body or away from it.*

John 14:2: *"In my father's house are many rooms; if it were not so, I would have told you. I am going there to prepare a place for you.*

2 Corinthians 12:9: *But he said to me, "My grace is sufficient for you, for my power is made perfect in weakness." Therefore I will boast all the more gladly about my weaknesses, so that Christ's power may rest on me.*

John 3:8: *The wind blows wherever it pleases. You hear its sound, but you cannot tell where it comes from or where it is going. So it is with everyone born of the spirit.*

Psalm 32:7: *You are my hiding place; you will protect me from trouble and surround me with songs of deliverance.*

Psalm 139:16: *Your eyes saw my unformed body. All the days ordained for me were written in your book before one of them came to be.*

Isaiah 61:3: *And to provide for those who grieve in Zion - to bestow on them a crown of beauty instead of ashes, the oil of gladness instead of mourning, and a garment of praise instead of a spirit of despair. They will be called oaks of righteousness, a planting of the Lord for the display of his splendor.*

Philippians 4:12: *I know what it is to be in need, and I know what it is to have plenty. I have learned the secret of being content in any and every situation, whether well fed or hungry, whether living in plenty or in want.*

Psalm 118:14: *The Lord is my strength and my song; he has become my salvation.*

Romans 5:3-5: *Not only so, but we also rejoice in our sufferings, because we know that suffering produces perseverance; perseverance, character; and character, hope. And hope does not disappoint us, because God has poured out his love into our hearts by the Holy Spirit, whom he has given us.*

Matthew 26:41: *"Watch and pray so that you will not fall into temptation. The Spirit is willing, but the body is weak."*

Matthew 6:33-34: *But seek first his kingdom and his righteousness and all these things will be given to you as well. Therefore do not worry about tomorrow, for tomorrow will worry about itself. Each day has enough trouble of its own.*

Psalm 27:14: *Wait for the Lord; be strong and take heart and wait for the Lord.*

Philippians 4:13: *I can do everything through him who gives me strength.*

1 Peter 5:7: *Cast your anxiety on him because he cares for you.*

Galatians 5:22: *But the Fruit of the Spirit is love, joy, peace, patience, kindness, goodness, faithfulness, gentleness and self control.*

Psalm 37:3-4: *Trust in the Lord, and do good; dwell in the land and enjoy safe pasture. Delight yourself in the Lord and He will give you the desires of your heart.*

Ephesians 5:31: *And the two will become one flesh.*

James 1:17: *Every good and perfect gift is from above, coming down from the Father of the heavenly lights, who does not change like shifting shadows.*

Joel 2:25: *I will repay you for the years the locusts have eaten.*

Mark 11:25: *"And when you stand praying, if you hold anything against anyone, forgive him, so that your father in heaven may forgive you your sins."*

Psalm 30:10-12: *Hear, O Lord, and be merciful to me; O Lord, be my help. You turned my wailing into dancing; you removed my sackcloth and clothed me with joy, that my heart may sing to you and not be silent. O Lord my God, I will give you thanks forever.*

Psalm 30:5: *Weeping may remain for a night, but rejoicing comes in the morning.*

John 3:8: *The wind blows wherever it pleases. You hear its sound, but you cannot tell where it comes from or where it is going. So it is with everyone born of the Spirit.*

Isaiah 43:19: *See I am doing a new thing! Now it springs up; do you not perceive it, I am making a way in the desert and streams in the wasteland.*

John 16:33: *I have told you these things so that in me you may have peace. In this world you will have trouble but take heart I have overcome the world.*

James 4:14: *Why, you do not even know what will happen tomorrow. What is your life? You are a mist that appears for a little while and then vanishes.*

Romans 8:28: *And we know that in all things God works for the good of those who love him, who have been called according to his purpose.*

Ecclesiastes 3:1-8: *"There is a time for everything, and a season for every activity under heaven: a time to be born and a time to die, a time to plant and a time to uproot, a time to kill and a time to heal, a time to tear down and a time to build, a time to weep and a time to laugh, a time to mourn and a time to dance, a time to scatter stones and a time to gather them, a time to* *embrace and a time to refrain, a time to search and a time to give up, a time to keep and a time to throw away, a time to tear and a time to mend, a time to be silent and a time to speak, a time to love and a time to hate, a time for war and a time for peace."*

John 3:16: *For God so loved the world that he gave his one and only Son, that whoever believes in him shall not perish but have eternal life.*

Luke 23:42-43: *Then he said, "Jesus, remember me when you come into your kingdom." Jesus answered him, "I tell you the truth, today you will be with me in paradise."*